DAVID HERZOG

GLORY AND THE END TIMES

UNVEILING GOD'S PROPHETIC VISION FOR YOUR FUTURE, ISRAEL, AND THE LAST-DAYS AWAKENING

DESTINY IMAGE® PUBLISHERS, INC.
PO Box 310, Shippensburg, PA 17257-0310
"Publishing cutting-edge prophetic resources to supernaturally empower the body of Christ"

This book and all other Destiny Image and Destiny Image Fiction books are available at Christian bookstores and distributors worldwide.

For more information on foreign distributors, call 717-532-3040.
Reach us on the Internet: www.destinyimage.com.

ISBN 13 TP: 979-8-8815-0386-4
ISBN 13 eBook: 979-8-8815-0387-1

For Worldwide Distribution, Printed in the USA
1 2 3 4 5 6 7 8 / 29 28 27 26 25

CONTENTS

FOREWORD

David Herzog has written a wonderful book on *Glory and the End Times*. Many know that on January 1, 1986, the Lord revealed to me the next 40 years. I have written several books about that. In that 40-year period, He said that He would determine who would have a hunger for His glory. When the Lord visited me with His glory and overwhelmed me with His glory in 1979, every cell of my body changed. The real war in the latter days will be for His glory.

Glory is linked with greatness, spaciousness, brightness, and being desired. Glory is linked with Jehovah and His expressions. Glory is linked with the weight and heaviness of wealth. Glory is linked with *you* (your self or soul). Glory is the manifestation of God through and to you. Glory is synonymous with dignity, abundance, wealth, treasure, splendor, brightness, majesty, perfection, Heaven's bliss, and giving Him reverence by speaking truth.

One of the greatest mysteries is Christ in you—*the hope of glory* (Colossians 1:27)! The will of God when He created man, planted a garden, and placed man in the garden, was for the glory to increase and cover the entire earth. Man was given the assignment to walk in the glory, find the glory in each element of creation, and cultivate and multiply that glory realm.

The voice of the serpent in the garden was the anti-force against God's Glory. How we detect curses today is when we recognize that the glory is diminishing or is absent in a person, territory, and nation. God Himself, Jehovah Yahweh, reveals who He is through signs, manifestations, and wonders, and presents Himself to us in His glory. His goal is for us to model after Him. This determines our human dignity, majesty, and glory. Psalm 16 says that each one of us carries a glory portion within us, and can fully reflect Him as we submit our entire being to Him.

Do we really understand the "Presence and Glory War"? A better way to approach this may be from an understanding of atmosphere. According to the American Dictionary of the English Language, *atmosphere* is the whole mass of fluid, consisting of air, aqueous and other vapors, surrounding the earth. Of course, the word comes from the interaction of vapor and sphere. Vapor is the fumes, moist floating substance, or an invisible elastic fluid that encompasses the earth's sphere. James 4:14 (NKJV) says, "*Whereas you do not know what will happen tomorrow. For what is your life? It is even a vapor that appears for a little time and then vanishes away.*"

We have an atmosphere about us that affects the way the earth operates. The atmosphere we carry affects the land we walk upon. Psalm 39:5 (NKJV) says, "*...Certainly every man at his best state is but vapor.*" The more we are in one with God and His purpose for the earth, the more we create a right atmosphere around us.

Glory and the End Times will assist you in having a desire to experience a great spiritual awakening and begin to move in glory and supernatural power. This book will help you understand the glory God planned for Israel in the days ahead. This book will help you understand your DNA and bloodline and how we are prone to resist His glory; but when we submit, His glory accelerates within us. This book will lead you into the highest dimension of seeking Father's Glory in your own life.

As children of God, part of our inheritance is experiencing the glory of God and being transformed into new levels of His glory. Each carries with it a particular blessing and thrill for us as Christians. To experience the glory of God is to experience His manifest presence. It is to go beyond an abstract understanding of His omnipresence to knowing that God Himself is there with us—with you, tangibly in your midst.

When God's manifest presence invades our daily lives, things change! We cannot remain the same. Either we will harden our hearts, as the Israelites did on many occasions, or we experience new *zoe* life. If we choose to allow God's presence to soften our hearts, we may see the power of God released in greater measure. We may catch a glimpse of the very atmosphere of Heaven. We experience God! He longs to pour out His glory upon His people so that we may know Him. This experience is not just for us personally, but for the harvest of souls the Lord would draw in through the magnetic influence His presence has on the lost.

There is a way to move from glory to glory. But why is it necessary to move from glory to glory? Isn't one glory as good as the next? *The answer is **no**,* because in every season of glory, we experience a new order that God brings to our lives as we mirror His image to a greater extent. And then we begin to add a new method—a settled plan or strategy of how we operate within that new order. It is our way of implementing what we have learned from God.

While in and of itself this is not a problem, we can eventually get so organized in God's last manifestation of glory that the enemy can use it to hold us back from God's next step for us. It is so easy to become legalistic or build binding doctrines around a truth that God revealed during a season of glory. That, however, can leave us open to not moving forward when it comes time for God to change the seasons in our lives.

If we do not allow God to move us from glory to glory, we will get caught up in living in an old season. As the Holy Spirit moves us toward becoming more Christlike, the methodology of an old season will not propel us into the future. We need something new and fresh. We need a new glory. David Herzog's book, *Glory and the End Times*, will keep you moving with a desire to step into a new realm of His glory.

Dr. Chuck D. Pierce
President, Glory of Zion International
Kingdom Harvest Alliance

1

AWAKENING OR BUST

We are at the point in world history that only a great spiritual awakening will save our nation and the nations of the world. The USA has been in a similar place before where the morality of the society was collapsing, crime and government corruption were rampant, and it looked like the end of Christianity in America. Then suddenly praying men and women helped to usher in a Great Awakening! The revival historian Dr. J. Edwin Orr gave a lecture describing the deplorable spiritual conditions in in 1776-1781, saying in part:

> Not many people realize that in the wake of the American Revolution (1776-1781) there was moral slump. Drunkenness became epidemic. Out of a population of five million, 300,000 were confirmed drunkards. Profanity was of the most shocking kind. For the first time in the history of the American settlement, women were afraid to go out at night for fear of assault. Bank robberies were a daily occurrence....[1]

Dr. Orr also stated:

> A poll taken at Harvard discovered not one believer in the student body. They took a poll at Princeton, a

> much more evangelical place, where they discovered only two believers in the student body, and only five that did not belong to the filthy speech movement of that day. Students held a mock communion at Williams College. They put on anti-Christian plays at Dartmouth and burned down Nassau Hall at Princeton. They took a Bible out of a local Presbyterian church in New Jersey and burnt it in a public bonfire. Christians were so few on campus in the 1790s that they met in secret and kept their minutes in code so that no one would know.[2]

Things got worse and worse until 1794 when conditions reached their very worst. Then suddenly the few Christians and pastors started to organize concerts of prayer to plead for the soul of the nation to be saved. Then in 1798, revival fires began to burn across New England and churches could not even keep up with those coming to ask about salvation!

This has been the history of revival and awakening in America! Across the nation when the level of depravity had reached its peak as the church lost its fire, believers once again cried out to God and God visited them with a burning, which affected society after affecting the church. In one area, people could not be elected to any type of government office unless they were proven born-again believers as no one would vote for them! In other towns, bars were closed as there was no one visiting the bars anymore.

In Wales the revival hit the coal miners so profoundly that jails were emptied and police officers were bored with no crime to take care of. And mules could no longer help work the coal mines because they were so used to being cursed at and kicked to obey orders that they no longer understood the change of vocabulary and actions and had to be retrained.

We talk often about changing this or that problem in the United States and create campaigns to stop this or that ungodly law affecting the seven mountains of society. But have you ever thought about the fact that when the Great Awakenings burned across America in the past, those social ills were suddenly vanquished. Even abolishing slavery had its roots in the Second Great Awakening!

Often the church and people try to solve human problems that can only be cured by a change of heart that comes from a spiritual awakening. It's hard to force godly laws on a population that no longer believes in the God of the Bible. But, once an awakening occurs, these are no longer an impossible mountain of obstacles.

We are at the point in America and the world that we need one more sweeping move of God, another Great Awakening, as nothing else will work at this point. If there is no awakening, we will lose our nation to evil. All the motivational steps, intellectual logic, and gimmicks have been exhausted. We must allow God to invade us and our nations once again to shift the tide of darkness taking over, then we will see millions and even billions of souls run back to Jesus.

We are on the verge of the last great spiritual awakening given the signs of the times. Satan knows his time is short, but we also know that we are to be *"redeeming the time, because the days are evil"* (Ephesians 5:16 NKJV).

Prayer and Fire

Atmospheric pressure causes rain. We can have the potential for awakening and revival and even prophetic words to back it up, but there needs to be a certain atmospheric pressure in the clouds to produce the rain. Just as we can know it's time for a great awakening and point to all the signs, we need to press in with prayer, repentance, fasting, and seeking His face in unity to increase the pressure in the spirit on the prophetic words of a final great awakening.

How do we know we are due for a final great awakening? All the signs point to the timing being now for a great shaking and a great awakening, which we will discuss throughout this book.

Every great move of God was preceded by huge prayer movements. Most the attention goes to the actual awakenings, moves, and revivals and those who were the primary speakers, but none of those moves of God would have happened if it was not for those who cried out to God in intense prayer for a season before the move started. When you research the great awakenings in America, they were all preceded by great prayer movements and crying out to God due to the spiritual void and depravity of their day. Today we see major prayer and fasting movements unlike anything we have seen before—but much more is coming!

It's true that you cannot force God to bring a move of God, but you can surely position yourself in prayer, repentance, fasting, and worship that creates a landing strip for the move of God. Nothing happens without prayer. And when we pray, we ask God to search our hearts as we repent anything in our lives that is not of God. Repentance always starts in people's hearts, then in the church, then spreads out to the world.

> *If My people who are called by My name will humble themselves, and pray and seek My face, and turn from their wicked ways, then I will hear from heaven, and will forgive their sin and heal their land* (2 Chronicles 7:14 NKJV).

It's not our job to point out all the evil in world, but it is to first repent of our own sin and apathy as individuals and as a church and ask for the fire of God to come burn in us once again. After we do this, the fire will return.

When you first believed in Jesus, you probably freely shared the gospel and your testimony of what Jesus did for you with friends and family—not fearing what they would think as your life was changed! You would read the Bible with awe and enjoy spending time with Jesus praying and soaking in His presence. Why? Because there was a fire burning in your heart. Maybe some years have gone by since your first encounter with Jesus and salvation, and the fire is waning.

Sharing Jesus

When was the last time you started sharing Jesus with people and asking if you could pray for them to know Jesus or pray for their healing or give a prophetic word to a lost soul? Could it be that the fire is not burning in you as it once was? Has sin, apathy, worldliness, entertainment, fear of rejection or persecution, and the approval of the world choked out the fire of the Holy Spirit in your life?

This is the state of much of the church in the Western world. People get overly concerned with what people might think if they share Jesus, and by fearing rejection, they have allowed the spirit of the world to invade them. How do you get that fire back? Repent and ask God to fill you once again with His Holy Spirit and fire until it burns so deeply you can't stop sharing Him with everyone. It all starts with prayer, repentance, and waiting on God to fill you with the fire of the Holy Spirit!

The truth is, once you've known the glory and power and fire of God and then you go back to lukewarm, you are never really truly satisfied with anything else. This in turn produces frustrated and critical believers who are not willing to go all-in for Jesus, and they criticize and attack others who attempt to burn bright for Jesus. We need to be refilled with the Holy Spirit just as the apostles were in Acts 2 and then again in Acts 4. Each level brought with it a new outpouring that was greater and greater.

Jesus had told the apostles and disciples to tarry in Jerusalem and pray and wait for the outpouring of the Holy Spirit during the Jewish feast of Pentecost. The custom for Jews during Pentecost was always to read the Scriptures and pray, but this time was different. Jesus promised that the Holy Spirit would come after His departure. They pressed in for days praying, fasting, meditating on the promises of God and waiting. They positioned themselves for a visitation. Then suddenly the Holy Spirit filled them up. This resulted in a new fire, power, and boldness to share the gospel as the church grew and souls were added daily!

But then in Acts chapter 4, it seems they were in need of boldness and fearlessness again as they prayed for boldness and then shared the gospel despite the threats and persecution. This second wave of Holy Spirit fire, power, and infilling created even greater results! When they went out again after this new outpouring, the Bible says the number of believers had multiplied! And they were not only just laying hands on the sick, but Peter's shadow alone would heal the sick. Those who had mocked them before now were fearful to join them. And no one lacked anything among them! Prayer, repentance, worship, and waiting on the Lord positioned them for an even greater harvest of souls with greater power and boldness!

I'm convinced that most believers, including those who claim to be Spirit-filled, need a fresh outpouring of the Holy Spirit and with fire. If believers are fearful to share their faith in public, while never seeing the power of Jesus in operation outside of church meetings, and have weak prayers lives relying on natural gifts and gifts of the Holy Spirit rather than intimacy with Jesus that brings the glory presence and power of God around them—this all points to the fact that the fire is missing!

Fire Spreads

Fire spreads naturally. If you have fire, you don't need to be prodded to share once a month with your church or pass out tracts, it just bubbles out of you as an overflow with people you meet naturally daily and weekly.

Water refreshes, but it's fire that spreads. "*...He will baptize you with the Holy Spirit and fire*" (Matthew 3:11 NKJV). Many believers mistake the refreshing of the presence of the Holy Spirit with the fire of the Holy Spirit! The fire convicts you of sins both big and small and purges it out of you as you let it burn through you till it's only Jesus speaking and acting through you, where you allow Jesus to borrow your mouth and hands to speak and pray for people.

Fear of man is burned out of you, and sharing the gospel becomes just as natural as talking and breathing. Let Him fully take you over so you can be a mouthpiece and river of life to revive a dying world.

We are our own biggest obstacle. When we get out of the way and are not concerned with what people think to the point where we believe "*it is no longer I who live, but Christ lives in me*" (Galatians 2:20 NKJV), then we are suddenly flowing in the rivers of personal revival and awakening. There is no great awakening or revival without prayer, repentance, and the outpouring of the Holy Spirit.

There is no great awakening or revival without prayer, repentance, and the outpouring of the Holy Spirit.

Even in the natural there is no harvest without rain. Some are trying to get a harvest from last season's rain (revival). We need a fresh rain if we want to see a fresh harvest! Millions are dying in sin and don't know Jesus. But it takes more than just willpower to share and see the lost saved. Something needs to change in us to where it flows naturally with a glory and power that emanates from us, drawing the lost even before we open our mouth to share.

We need to cry out to God for an outpouring of the Holy Spirit and His fire! A new rain will bring a new harvest.

The Word of God says in Romans 3:23, *"all have sinned and fall short of the glory of God."* Because it is true that every human lost the glory, meaning somehow they knew the glory at some point, then it's also true when the Glory of God returns, it draws sinners back to God. If every human lost the Glory of God, then when they are in the glory presence of God, it draws them back to Him. They start to realize this is what they were looking and longing for all along.

How could every human have lost the Glory of God unless they first experienced the glory? Let me explain how.

Home Again

Jeremiah 1:5 speaks about God knowing us and calling us before we were in our mother's womb. *That means we knew God in His glory in Heaven as a spirit before we were formed in our mother's womb on earth*. We spend a lifetime trying to find what will satisfy us only to realize that who we need is Jesus, Heaven, and the Glory of God!

I have seen so many people get saved who had never heard the gospel—and when they got saved they said they felt like they were home again. But how could it have been home if they had never experienced Jesus or gone to church and had grown up in a totally unreached nation. It was because the spirit that God puts in us is on a nonstop search for God from where we all first emanated. It's like being in a remote place as your phone is nonstop searching for a WiFi signal. That's how most people go through life searching for anything that will satisfy until they find Jesus and realize that's who they were looking for all along without realizing it.

I remember preaching in Paris, France, in a revival that went for six months straight! When I was initially invited, I asked the pastor if he would organize a fasting and prayer chain for 40 days prior to my coming. At first he said there was no need as they were not too keen on fasting. I told the pastor if that was the case, then there was no need for me to come preach if they only wanted to maintain the atmosphere that was already there. I told him that if he was willing to ask 40 people to each take one day consecutively to fast and pray for a move of God, then I would come and was certain God would show up in a new way.

Finally, they decided to fast and form a prayer chain prior to the meetings. The revival that was supposed to last five days became six months. Each night new souls were saved, people repented of sin and brought articles of sin to the altar, including pornography, objects of witchcraft, and other such things. Miraculous healings took place and huge deliverances from demonic bondages abounded.

During the first week of the revival, I prophesied that France would win the World Soccer Cup as a sign of the favor of God on France at that time. It turned out France beat Brazil 3-0, and the pastor decided this was a sign to keep the revival going for six months. It was the most amazing time. Atheists and Muslims were easily saved, lukewarm and backslidden Christians wept at the altar repenting and returning to Jesus as people came from all over France and other nearby nations to attend the revival. The atmosphere was like days of Heaven on earth in one of the darkest spiritual nations and cities in the Western world. Once God shows up, nothing is impossible!

Another time, I was asked to speak in Denver, Colorado, for four nights. I had sensed as well as the pastor that this timing might get extended. I asked the pastor to set up a fasting chain to prepare the area for an extended move of God. Little did we realize at the time that the revival would continue for eight weeks! We saw many souls saved, amazing miracles, and crazy deliverances. One man was healed of third-degree burns just as he walked into the foyer before even entering the meeting place.

On the third day, a sorcerer claiming to be the third-highest sorcerer of Boulder, Colorado, one hour away. He was walking around the outside of the church speaking curses. When invited in, he said he was sent from the number one and second-highest sorcerers in Boulder, which was about 30 miles away. He explained that the revival was hindering their ability to do things in the demonic realm that they were able to do before. They seemed to be experiencing a "disturbance in the force," so to speak. He refused to come inside, claiming he feared he could drop dead if he walked in where the meeting was occurring.

At the beginning of the revival, we found decapitated animals on the church property. One night I challenged the satanists who had killed a poor cat as a sacrifice for demonic power that it was no match for our sacrifice, Jesus Christ, who died and was resurrected. I asked the satanists to compare the sacrifice of Jesus with the sacrifices of dead animals and say which was more powerful! Jesus' sacrifice, of course, was infinitely more powerful and life-changing compared to a dead cat. We started to see people in witchcraft, satanism, and Wicca become ever so curious at this "strange disturbance in the force" they were sensing—and some even got saved.

When the power of God is fully released, the enemy cannot stop it. We only lose when we don't activate the full power of God at our disposal. The blood of Jesus is the most powerful weapon and message, yet it's the least-used weapon and the least talked about. It is time to fully activate the power of the blood of Jesus, which is what saves the world!

Men of God Full of Holy Spirit Power

Reinhard Bonnke was one of the most powerful and effective evangelists in Africa, seeing the largest crusades in history—up to 1 million people in one service with the most salvations in recorded history.

Bonnke's secret is revealed in one of his first books, titled *Evangelism by Fire*. He calls it "Battering Rams" of prayer. They would pray and fast and intercede with such an intensity and fire before and during the outdoor crusades that the demonic atmosphere of witchcraft and unbelief would shift and hundreds of thousands would be saved in a single night. This went on for decades, and his ministry continues today via his spiritual sons! Witch doctors and government leaders alike gave their hearts to Jesus. The most amazing creative miracles and even resurrections would occur during the meetings.

Due to these moves of God in Africa through the prayer and preaching of Reinhard Bonnke, much of Africa now is considered one of the most Christian nations and continents on the planet.

Charles G. Finney was one of the most effective and powerful revivalists in American history. His secret was to have high-level intercessors go into the towns weeks before, and there hole up in a room praying and fasting. Then when Finney would come to preach, the atmosphere was open and the people's hearts were softened to receive salvation. The main intercessors he sent ahead were Daniel Nash and Brother Abel Clary who went into towns to prepare the way. Charles Finney only stopped his revival work after his main intercessor, Daniel Nash, passed away. That says a lot about how much Finney depended on his intercessors. Without prayer there's no revival or awakening, but with prayer all things are possible to those who believe.

Often when Finney entered a place, amazing things would occur, including entire factories shutting down and the men working would repent and cry out to God for salvation. How did he do this? Was it the way he worded his sermons? No, it was the ardent prayer before and behind the scenes.

In his early revivals, Finney would mention that when "the people were threatening me" and "were full of wrath," he agreed with a deacon to spend the whole day in fasting and prayer. "Just at evening the Lord gave us great enlargement and promise of victory." After earnest preaching to a full house, the next day, "I found a state of wonderful conviction of sin and alarm for their souls."[3]

Finney writes further:

> In regard to my own experience, I will say that unless I had the spirit of prayer I could do nothing. If even for a

> day or an hour I lost the spirit of grace and supplication, I found myself unable to preach with power and efficiency, or win souls by personal conversation. I found myself having more or less power in preaching, and in personal labors for souls, just in proportion as I had the spirit of prevailing prayer. I have found that unless I kept myself and have been kept in such relations to God as to have daily and hourly access to him in prayer, my efforts to win souls were abortive; but that when I could prevail with God in prayer, I could prevail with man in preaching, exhortation, and conversation.[4]

Jesus' Cross of Sacrifice

When I do large outdoor stadium events like the one I did recently in Pakistan where we saw nearly 1 million salvations, huge prayer is behind it! It was two different cities two nights in a row with over 500,000 unsaved Muslims in each outdoor evangelistic campaign. On the ground, thousands prepared in long fasts, up to 40 days, among the pastors, leaders, and church members. The utter desperate prayers for their nation and cities to be saved along with an amazing team that knew how to organize such events made all the difference in the world. In this crusade the people were saved by the simple but very conviction message of salvation from sin, hell, and the only way to salvation and Father God is through the Cross and sacrifice of Jesus. Then the salvation call was overwhelming! Shortly after, the miracles exploded as I have never seen so many blind eyes opened as in those meetings, along with paralytics walking, mute speaking, demon possessed set free, and so many other miracles.

Apart from fasting and praying myself before the crusades, each time in my hotel I can feel the overwhelming pressure and responsibility—and I must have a breakthrough in prayer or I feel useless. I feel like what women describe as being in labor, feeling such pressure and discomfort to where it drives me to keep pressing in until I feel the release and breakthrough. Once I get that release from the pressure and the burden as it finally lifts, then I know all is good and everything will flow perfectly.

One interesting note is that most places that see such crowds and miracles on a consistent basis are also nations in great need. Pakistan is very needy both materially and spiritually, as most people are extremely poor and many live under Islam. They don't know anything else, as many in the Christian church experience extreme persecution. Yet despite all this and sometimes due to these factors, the glory, harvest, and power of God is showcased even greater!

Could it be that in God's mercy He may allow some of our idols to be shaken or smashed, such as materialism, love of money, fame and greed and overeating and indulgences, causing many to suddenly snap out of their daze and come to their senses and run to the Lord?

When 9/11 occurred, I remember there was a huge surge in interest in Jesus, prayer, and going to church; the churches were full for a few months with many unsaved, even atheists and backsliders. Though the surge was short-lived, it showed that when life is tough in the natural, many then run to the Lord for salvation. Often when we pray for loved ones to be saved and for the Lord to use whatever means necessary to bring them to Himself, they will go though some very difficult circumstances, causing them to cry out to God. They eventually come to the Lord, especially if they are stubborn or hardened against the gospel.

Both the goodness of God and the fear of the Lord can lead to repentance. In America, we have had the goodness of God on our land and we have seen great moves of God, but I believe the shaking and the holy reverence and fear of the Lord is also about to come to our land to cause many to awaken from their spiritual stupor and cry out once again to the Lord!

The USA, like many Western nations, is in a spiritual state like Samson. Once greatly used by God, the US and many nations' spiritual eyes and senses have been gouged out and are now in a form of spiritual oppression and slavery to the enemy. Suddenly in such a low place, Samson cried out to God to use him one more time, realizing the error of his ways. God in His mercy heard his cry and used him one last time! In fact, God used Samson more that one last time than any other time in his life as he pushed the two pillars holding up the entire Philistine nation, taking down all their rules, the elites, magicians, and the source of their demonic power in one fell swoop!

Could it be that God is giving America and many other nations one last chance to be used by Him, greater now than at any other time in our history? And not because we deserve it, but because of God's mercy—as a remnant has been crying out for mercy and repentance even in a time of judgments on earth. The best is yet to come!

2

LORD OF HOSTS

One of the end-time glory tools that God is now using and will release more and more is the Lord of Hosts, also known as the Angel Armies. These are not your normal angels that minister to the heirs of salvation. These are like the nuclear option to take down some of the highest levels of giants in the spirit. These Angel Armies will be unleashed more and more as we progress into the most exciting and challenging season of the end times.

There are different types of angelic beings, and these are some of the most powerful. These types of angelic hosts are mentioned approximately 290 times in the Bible—nearly ten times the sum of all others referenced in the Bible. Additionally, the context of literally hundreds of Scriptures includes the meaning of this awesome revelation of God. It's not just a category of angels, it's also one of God's names. When we use a name of God in battle or prayer, that is often how the Lord will manifest Himself. For example, when we call out to Jehovah Rapha our Healer, He heals.

So what is this name of God we can use in battle that can overcome some of the most powerful end-time demonic beings?

Let me introduce you to *Yahweh-Sabaoth,* the Lord of Hosts. From the sheer number of references alone, we see that the Lord of Armies is the revelation of God's name as one of the most frequently unveiled to humankind in the Bible. Yet it is hardly ever preached on or expounded upon. Could it be God is saving this for when we will need it the most to see God manifest on our behalf as Lord of the Angel Armies? He is the Captain of the Lord of Hosts. He has been called Commander and Chief of the Lord's armies. Check out Joshua 5:13-15 where Christ appears to Joshua as the Commander of the Lord's armies. I believe that God's Armies of Angels fight on our behalf against principalities and powers and wickedness in high places. Psalm 24:10 (KJV) and Luke 2:13-14 (KJV) both speak of the heavenly hosts being angels and praising God, the King of glory.

Jesus manifests in the way we perceive Him, worship Him, and call upon Him. The more we expand our revelation of Him in the glory, the more access to God we have and can operate in. Some churches only have a revelation of salvation but not healing, so they call on the God of salvation and see those results of souls saved. But they may not see other aspects of God's nature and names like Healer, Deliverer, Provider, etc. Let's keep expanding our revelation of Him to have the fullness of what He paid for on the Cross!

When we talk about fighting for our personal transformation or warring for our families, cities, and nation, it is the Lord of Hosts we want to follow into battle.

The Lord of Hosts met Joshua on the plains of Jericho (Joshua 5:14); and it was the God of Angel Armies who led David into battle against the Philistines. David said in 1 Samuel 17:45 (NKJV): "*...I come to you in the name of the Lord of hosts...*" (Angel Armies). That declaration resulted in a giant going down and all of Israel being saved—and an entire nation going from defense to offense both in the natural and the spiritual realms!

David had a revelation to be a giant killer, as long as he operated with the Captain of the Lord of Hosts.

Use the Name of the Lord of Hosts in Battle

When surrounded by your enemies that seem overwhelming, God can come as the Lord of Hosts!

In 2 Kings 6, Elisha, a prophet and successor to Elijah, encounters an extraordinary event. The king of Syria, Ben-Hadad, sends a large army to capture Elisha, who was residing in Dothan, a city in Israel. Elisha's servant, who was with him, became frightened as he saw the vast Syrian army surrounding them.

In response, Elisha prays to the Lord, asking Him to open his servant's eyes to see the spiritual reality. The Lord answers Elisha's prayer, and the servant's eyes are opened. He beholds an army of angels, consisting of horses and chariots of fire, surrounding them. This divine intervention reassures the servant of God's power and presence.

Elisha then prays for the Syrian army to be struck with blindness, and the Lord grants his request. The Syrian soldiers, unable to see, stumble and lose their way. Elisha leads them away from Dothan, guiding them to Samaria in Israel. Once inside the city, Elisha asks the Lord to restore the soldiers' sight, and they are able to see again. (See 2 Kings 6:15-23.)

The first time I believe the Lord opened my eyes to see the Angel Armies of the Lord of Hosts was during a 22,000-person crusade in Mexico City in 2019. Masses were saved and some of the most amazing miracles occurred with the most powerful testimonies I had seen to that date and mass deliverances as well.

Suddenly during the worship I could see huge angelic beings unlike anything I had ever seen before. They were very fierce looking, not the kind you would want to have a conversation with. Their presence with Jesus as the Lord of Hosts in full power, caused such an overwhelming presence of God's Glory and also an intensity in the Spirit that is hard to describe.

Even in the green room after an event when we were just fellowshipping, the glory entered and became so strong that all the speakers, including me, the staff, helpers, and young kids, suddenly began weeping and we were overcome by the Spirit of God. I started to notice the Angelic Hosts more and more, especially in some of our larger epic stadium-type of events where we needed it most.

As mentioned in the previous chapter, I have been conducting large crusades in Pakistan, seeing over 500,00 unsaved Muslims show up at one time. That is a place I really need the Lord of Hosts to show up! Every time I call on Him in this way using this name of God, He shows up big time! For example, the last time I did an open-air crusade, preaching to over 1 million unsaved in two nights, it felt like I was a spectator watching it all. I reached over 1 million souls in those two nights, as most easily responded to the salvation call in those two nights and that was *before* any miracles had occurred, which shocked me as usually we see that miracles lead to salvations.

The simple convicting gospel message caused such a deep cry for salvation before any miracles occurred that I was astounded at the response. Then the power of God exploded as many blind eyes opened, paralytics walked, mute and deaf were speaking and hearing, totally demon-possessed people were set free, and all were testifying on stage! I have seen these miracles many times before, but it was the ease and speed that amazed me.

The Captain of the Lord of Hosts along with His Angel Armies were in full manifestation in Pakistan, and it was the same in Mexico City, and now many of the other 70 nations where I have preached. There is a certain realm of glory that I just know is there when these city- and nation-changing Hosts of Heaven show up. The presence is a game changer!

Lepers in Syrian Camp

According to the biblical account in 2 Kings 7:3-11, four men with leprosy wandered into a Syrian camp only to find it deserted. The Syrians had fled in a state of panic, believing that the king of Israel had hired the kings of the Hittites and the Egyptians to attack them. The lepers discovered that the Lord had caused the Syrians to hear the noise of chariots and horses, leading them to believe they were under attack.

While the biblical account does not explicitly state that angelic hosts caused the Syrians to flee, it does mention that the Lord was involved in the events that unfolded, which I do believe was the Lord showing up as the Lord of Hosts with all those hosts of angelic beings.

In another biblical story, in 2 Kings 19:35, it is written that the angel of the Lord went out and killed 185,000 Assyrian army soldiers in a single night. This is the level of power these angelic hosts carry.

When the lepers entered the Syrian camp, they found it abandoned, with horses and donkeys still tied up, and tents still standing. They took advantage of the situation and began to plunder the camp, eating and drinking, and carrying away silver, gold, and clothing. Eventually, they decided to report their discovery to the king's household, leading to the people of the city going out and spoiling the tents of the Syrians. (See 2 Kings 7:3-20.)

Jesus' Angelic Legion Claim

According to the Bible, specifically in Matthew 26:53 (NASB), Jesus says, "*Or do you think that I cannot appeal to my Father, and He will at once put at My disposal more than twelve legions of angels?*" In this context, Jesus is responding to Peter's attempt to defend Him with a sword, saying, "*Put your sword back into its place...for all who draw the sword will die by the sword*" (Matthew 26:52 NIV). Jesus then notes that He could call upon His Father to send a vast army of angels to His aid, exceeding twelve legions (estimated to be around 72,000 angels, based on a Roman legion's typical size).

So these are military-type angels as He was using a Roman military term to describe these "legions" of angelic beings that He could call on if He wanted to. Of course, He chose not to as He knew He needed to die on the Cross to take away the sin of the world to make a way for salvation.

Jesus releases His power at higher levels to believers and ministers who walk in obedience to Him. The more God can trust us with a small amount of power and authority we operate in now, the more He will trust us with later.

Jesus says in Matthew 28:18 (NASB), "*All authority in heaven and on earth has been given to Me,*" and Matthew 10:1 (NASB) says, "*Jesus summoned His twelve disciples and gave them authority over unclean spirits, to cast them out, and to heal every disease and every sickness.*"

As Jesus shines more and more in us and God is saving the best for last, don't you think God is reserving levels of His power and authority in these end times of glory to demonstrate the full authority Jesus has? We are His hands and feet on earth. Jesus could command wind and waves and they obeyed, and He rebuked the disciples for their lack of faith during that storm as they screamed out in fear, awakening Him. Jesus had to wake up and do it Himself; I believe God wanted the disciples to exercise the authority He had released to them.

I remember in January 2020 we had a large stadium event in Phoenix, Arizona. In fact, it was to be the only mass stadium event in America that year due to the pandemic that hit shortly afterward. We rented the 50,000 seat Arizona State University football field. In addition to my wife, Stephanie, and me speaking, we had other amazing world-renown speakers, including evangelists, apostles, prophets, A-list, born-again singers and musicians known in both the secular and Christian world, and even the president and vice president of the Navajo nation.

Thousands were saved, healed, and set free, and it was televised both on Christian and local secular TV. The warfare hit 24 hours before the event at a level I had never encountered in my entire 30 years of ministry up to that point. We called on the God of Angel Armies to intervene, and miraculously the event went on without a hitch even though just before the enemy tried to bring chaos.

Not only did God show up big time, I had the opportunity to preach the gospel to millions on *Fox News* live as they had interviewed me asking about the event. And God paid for it all, which was another great miracle as it happened just in the final moments when it had to happen. It was so supernatural beyond anything I had ever seen before.

God wants souls saved, healed and delivered, and God wants to be worshipped in every place—in the stadiums, media, television, and in the entertainment world. He is a jealous God in the good sense, and He deserves to be worshipped instead pop stars, actors, celebrities, and politicians. Jesus alone is the Captain of the Lord of Hosts and the only Superstar, the Son of God and Savior of the world, deserving the right to be worshipped.

3

WARS AND REVIVALS LINKED

The glory and the end times are connected to what occurs in Israel. As it goes with Israel in the natural, so it goes with the church and the world in the spiritual realm.

Israel was not much of a topic for 2,000 years until Israel was reborn as a nation in 1948. What happened in 1948 after Israel became a nation with the full approval and help of the United States? The healing revivals began to be birthed across America! As Israel was being restored, God was restoring what the early church lost, the demonstration of the healing power of God.

The following are some of what was birthed:

- Los Angeles Crusade (1946-1949): William Branham's healing campaign in Los Angeles, California, marked the beginning of the Healing Revival in America. This event drew large crowds and sparked a wave of similar healing campaigns across the country. (This parallels the time of Israel's independence as a nation.)
- Latter Rain Movement (late 1940s to mid-1950s): The Healing Revival was closely tied to the Latter Rain Movement,

which emerged in western Canada after Branham's sermon. The movement spread internationally, attracting many of the same people participating in the Healing Revival. Prominent leaders, including Joseph Mattsson-Boze, played key roles in publicizing both movements through his magazine, *Herald of Faith*. (Again this is during the time the USA stood with Israel in the United Nations to form the reborn nation of Israel.)

- Multiple Healing Campaigns (1950s): By the mid-1950s, dozens of ministers associated with Branham and his campaigns had launched similar healing campaigns across America. This proliferation of healing revivals reached its peak in 1956, with 49 separate evangelists holding major meetings across the USA.

Another event happened after 1948. Billy Graham's first major crusade was held in Los Angeles in 1949, which gained him widespread attention and launched his evangelistic ministry. Over the years, Graham's crusades reached millions of people in 185 countries and territories on six continents, with an estimated 215 million people attending his crusades in person or via satellite feeds.

In 1967, Israel retook their capital of Jerusalem, which was a major end-time prophetic event triggering amazing spiritual blessings to the church! The well-known Jesus Movement exploded on the scene during this time as reflected in the movie *Jesus Revolution*. The movie showcased how many drugged-out hippies found Jesus and the gospel began spreading like wildfire!

Actually three parallel movements occurred during this time (late 1960s and early 1970s), including the Charismatic Movement (reaching Catholics, Anglicans, Methodists, Presbyterians, etc.) and the Jesus Movement, starting on the West Coast that also spread across the nation. But many don't know about the third historic movement—the Messianic Movement! This is the first time in 2,000 years that large numbers of Jewish believers received their Messiah in numbers not seen since the time of Jesus and the book of Acts!

Why then? Because every time Israel is restored physically, step by step the church is restored, including the movement of born-again Jewish believers!

Another amazing first-time event that occurred in the late 1960s is that the USA landed the first men on the moon. And on July 20, 1969, American astronaut Neil Armstrong walked on the moon. Could it be that God allowed America this miraculous journey into space because the USA stood by Israel and its right to its homeland and its capital of Jerusalem so it could one day host the return of their Messiah, Yeshua?

Israel's Restoration and the Church's Blessing: Romans 11:26 promises that *"all Israel will be saved."* As Israel is restored, the church will also experience spiritual blessings and restoration of what was lost since the early church. This restoration will not be limited to physical Israel but will encompass spiritual Israel, comprising both believing Jews and Gentiles (Romans 2:28-29).

1991 Iraq War, Israel, Toronto Blessing Parallels

The 1991 Gulf War and the Toronto Blessing, a Christian revival movement, may seem unrelated at first glance. However, upon closer examination, some intriguing parallels emerge.

Israel was attacked by Iraq, then the US along with a coalition of other mostly European nations retaliated and attacked Iraq.

The following are some of the parallels:

- Spiritual Awakening: Both the Gulf War and the Toronto Blessing were marked by a sense of spiritual awakening. The Gulf War saw a surge in prayer and spiritual seeking among Christians worldwide, and the Toronto Blessing was characterized by intense, uncontrollable laughter, weeping, and feelings of joy and freedom, often accompanied by physical manifestations such as shaking and falling.
- Global Reach: The Gulf War involved a global coalition of nations, and the Toronto Blessing spread rapidly around the globe, with thousands of people from diverse backgrounds and denominations experiencing the phenomenon.
- Unpredictability: The Gulf War's outcome was uncertain, with many fearing a prolonged and bloody conflict. Similarly, the Toronto Blessing's manifestations were unpredictable and uncontrollable, leaving many participants and observers wondering about their meaning and significance.
- Renewal and Revival: The Gulf War marked a turning point in international relations with the defeat of Iraq and the liberation of Kuwait. The Toronto Blessing, too, was seen as a catalyst for spiritual renewal and revival, with many participants reporting deepened faith and a sense of spiritual refreshment.
- Media Attention: Both events received extensive media coverage. The Gulf War was broadcast live around the world, and the Toronto Blessing was widely reported in newspapers, magazines, and television programs.

- Controversy and Criticism: The Gulf War was criticized for its humanitarian costs and the use of military force. The Toronto Blessing also faced criticism from some quarters not understanding some of the manifestations of laughter or falling in the spirit, while others claimed a lack of theological grounding.
- Long-term Impact: The first Gulf War had significant long-term consequences, including the containment of Saddam Hussein's regime and the establishment of a new regional balance of power. The Toronto Blessing contributed to a broader renewal of evangelical Christianity in the 1990s and beyond. Many ministers and ministries say this renewal saved their ministries and spiritual life from being burned out; they were at the point of quitting but turned to find the Father's love and experienced a new rebirth in their life and ministry.

This is not to say that the Iraq war was good or bad, as all war is hell. But what we can see here is when wars occur in Israel and nations like the USA come to defend Israel, it seems to be a trigger for spiritual movement in the US. That's because as Israel takes back its God-given land and territory, the church often referred to as "spiritual Israel" starts to also take back spiritual territory that it had lost over the past 2,000 years.

> *Now if their stumbling (their lapse, their transgression) has so enriched the world [at large], and if [Israel's] failure means such riches for the Gentiles, think what an enrichment and greater advantage will follow their full reinstatement!* (Romans 11:12 AMPC)

> *For if their rejection and exclusion from the benefits of salvation were [overruled] for the reconciliation of a world to God, what will their acceptance and admission mean? [It will be nothing short of] life from the dead!* (Romans 11:15 AMPC)

As Israel is restored more and more both physically and spiritually, it becomes as a resurrection for the church!

On the flip side, if the USA, or any other nation, comes against Israel and its right to its God-given land, it will cause a curse instead of a blessing to our nation. Books have been written clearly detailing the cause and effects of when the USA went against Israel in a wrong way, causing disasters in the USA often within 24 hours, including hurricanes, economy downturns, president's secret lives exposed, and natural disasters such as Hurricane Katrina in 2005 that occurred shortly after the USA pressured Israel to give up Gaza—which God has clearly given to Israel as revealed in the Bible.

To this day Gaza has been a thorn in Israel's side and the people living there have greatly suffered at the hands of the terror group Hamas ruling that area. Almost two years after October 7, 2023 when Hamas attacked Israel—killing more than 1,100 innocent people and brutally taking more than 200 hostages—Hamas in Gaza has been almost totally destroyed in retaliation for the attack.

As I write this, Israel is once again being forced to take back and control parts of Gaza, southern Lebanon, and parts of Syria just past the Golan Heights due to unprovoked attacks and threats by these nations since October 7, 2023.

Each time Israel takes back land in a war, it causes a huge spiritual advance for the church! Could it be that we are on the verge of possibly the greatest move of God that could come in the form of mass repentance, masses of souls saved, and a fresh outpouring of the Holy Spirit? As Israel is taking back land that God has promised to Israel, God is also having the church take back spiritual land that was lost in past decades. And amazingly, as Israel is taking back God-given land due to security issues, the USA is talking about possibly buying Greenland and taking back the Panama Canal, also for security reasons due to fear of upcoming wars with Russia and China. Whether this occurs or not remains to be seen, but the similarities are striking to even talk about the possibility.

We have ministered in Israel more these past few years than any other year, even during a time of war! The past 12 months (2024) as these events are occurring, we have seen more souls saved worldwide than any other year of my 34 years in full-time ministry! Could there be a parallel?

There is a future war Israel wins that will also cause and trigger a major move of God. This is the war of Gog and Magog. The spiritual awakening takes place right after this war as told in Ezekiel 39:29 (NKJV): "*'And I will not hide My face from them anymore; for I shall have poured out My Spirit on the house of Israel,' says the Lord God.*" God said the end of the Gog Magog War in the book of Ezekiel will trigger one of the greatest harvests of souls worldwide!

This is a season for believers and the church to make great advances while taking the ground and winning the lost. War is messy and so is spiritual awakening, revival, and soul winning. In fact, God is bringing a great shaking and cleansing in His people and the church at large. But the purpose is to purify His bride to get her ready. God is pruning His people to bear the greatest fruit and harvest! Could it be that the USA is like Samson who lost his way and his sight but at his lowest moment in prison, blind and bound he cried out to God for one more chance to make a difference!

Is God hearing the cry of His remnant in the USA and the nations and suddenly turning the tables and giving us one more chance to be a godly nation, see revival, and overturn the tables of the wicked? Just like Samson, many are praying, "Lord, give America (and many other nations) one more chance to fulfill its end-time destiny to be a nation that spreads the gospel and has one more great awakening!"

Mass repentance surely will be necessary, thus the reason for all the exposures and pruning occurring in the church. Could it be that God answers our prayers and America gets one more chance to be free enough to allow for one last great move of God while possibly being shaken economically. And we might not be the number one nation in terms of power, military, or economy forever; but maybe we become the last great move of God in the Western world, (The US is not clearly mentioned as an end-time player as are the nations of Israel, Iran, Russia, China, Europe.)

If the options are to be shaken as a nation but experience national repentance and revival—or stay a top nation but follow the antichrist agenda, I prefer we become a nation of revival, harvest, and spreading the gospel and become a sheep nation following our Good Shepherd once again!

A baby being born can be messy with screaming, loss of blood, weakening of the mother and complications, but the end result is great joy. I sense America is about to go through a great birthing that will shake and stretch many of us—but the end result will be something new being birthed in America and other nations worldwide.

Future End-Time Events Timeline

From what I see in the Word of God, there are several major end-time events and wars to look for to see how close we are to the future great harvest and advances in end-time glory as well as when the Lord returns! What you are about to read is very key as we are to be watchmen on the wall seeing what's coming.

The sons of Issachar had a gift of prophetical knowing what season they were in and what Israel needed to do at a specific time. The following are some things to pray and watch for.

Israel Defeats Neighboring Enemy Nations (Psalm 83)

Future wars are prophesied in the Bible. Now that we know every time Israel goes to war and wins and takes back land, there is a parallel in the spirit both for Israel and the nations. What we are witnessing right now is possibly the Psalm 83 war. In fact, Israel is fighting a war on seven fronts—being attacked on all sides but winning. In Psalm 83, Israel's neighbors are plotting to destroy the nation, as Hamas and Hezbollah (terrorist organizations set on destroying Israel) in Lebanon had planned to do on October 7, 2023.

The word *hamas* translates to "violence" in Hebrew. The Bible says in Isaiah 60:18 (AMPC), "*Violence* [hamas] *shall no more be heard in your land, nor devastation or destruction within your borders, but you shall call your walls Salvation and your gates Praise.*" Hamas breached the walls and gates and stormed into Israel killing, torturing, raping, and taking hostages of innocent Israelis living in peace near the wall. This verse is almost fully fulfilled because Hamas as an organized government and ministry virtually no longer exists in Gaza as all the leaders have been killed or fled and all their terror government structures have been destroyed. Some are trying to rule Gaza while living abroad, but Gaza has been reduced to rubble for the most part since the war.

In Psalm 83, Israel's neighbors are plotting to destroy the nation as Gaza and Hezbollah in Lebanon had planned to do on October 7, 2023. Their plan backfired as the terrorists in Gaza did not wait for the signal and went ahead of Hezbollah in Lebanon, wanting to get all the attention. Then Hezbollah attacked Israel with missiles every day after the attack.

Today, as of this writing, Hamas in Gaza is almost totally wiped out. Hezbollah in Lebanon is losing badly as all the senior leaders have been eliminated, as well as most of the lower ranking Hezbollah leaders. Israeli troops have advanced into southern Lebanon in Hezbollah territory. Other neighboring nations attacking Israel since October 7, 2023, were Syria, Iraq, Palestinian Territories, Yemen, and a lot farther away, Iran.

Let's look at Psalm 83 (NIV):

> *O God, do not remain silent; do not turn a deaf ear, do not stand aloof, O God. See how your enemies growl, how your foes rear their heads. With cunning they conspire against your people; they plot against those you cherish. "Come," they say, "let us destroy them as a nation, so that Israel's name is remembered no more."*
>
> *With one mind they plot together; they form an alliance against you—the tents of Edom and the Ishmaelites, of Moab and the Hagrites, Byblos, Ammon and Amalek, Philistia* [Gaza] *with the people of Tyre*

[Lebanon]. *Even Assyria* [Iraq and Syria] *has joined them to reinforce Lot's descendants.*

Do to them as you did to Midian, as you did to Sisera and Jabin at the river Kishon, who perished at Endor and became like dung on the ground. Make their nobles like Oreb and Zeeb, all their princes like Zebah and Zalmunna, who said, "Let us take possession of the pasturelands of God."

Make them like tumbleweed, my God, like chaff before the wind. As fire consumes the forest or a flame sets the mountains ablaze, so pursue them with your tempest and terrify them with your storm. Cover their faces with shame, Lord, *so that they will seek your name.*

May they ever be ashamed and dismayed; may they perish in disgrace. Let them know that you, whose name is the Lord*—that you alone are the Most High over all the earth.*

Mass Migration to Israel During Peace and Prosperity

As Israel defeats the terrorists and regions attacking Israel near its borders, a season of peace and prosperity will occur. As Israel is defeating its enemies, Jewish people are being attacked and blamed in the nations as anti-Semitism and anti-Jewish attacks are on a huge upswing in Europe, the USA, Australia, and other Western nations. This will only increase and cause a huge wave of more Jews immigrating to Israel from the nations!

Many French Jews moved to Israel in the early 2000s as great persecution of Jewish French citizens and vandalism of Jewish synagogues occurred so much that the French police had to station police at Jewish schools and synagogues. As wars increase with Israel and surrounding nations—yet all the while Israel experiences more peace and prosperity—many more Jews will desire to make *aliyah,* meaning immigrate to the land of their ancestors while in a season of peace, protection, and prosperity for a season in Israel.

Isaiah 17 Destruction of Damascus

Isaiah 17:1 (NKJV) says, *"The burden against Damascus: 'Behold, Damascus will cease from being a city, and it will be a ruinous heap.'"* This is a key turning point in end-time prophecy for Israel and the nations and is a key signpost to look for.

In December 2024, rebels suddenly took over Syria and Damascus as the leader, President Bashar Assad, fled to Russia to seek asylum. This dictator had been in power for more than 50 years, yet in just 10 days of fighting, the power structure flipped. This was a huge shift.

The rebels that took over claim to be moderates, but their leader was part of al-Qaeda (enemy of Israel and US) and ISIS (notorious terrorist group) flags were seen on their vehicles. They have been executing Syrians who worked for the former government without a trial or confirming that they were part of the former government. They have declared on some videos that they will next take over Jerusalem and Mecca.

For many years prior, I wondered how and why Damascus would be wiped out so suddenly as it is one of oldest continually inhabited nations on earth. The former leader, Assad, was wise enough not to try to interfere or attack Israel since the 1973 Yom Kippur war.

Suddenly the tables have changed! Partly because Israel weakened Iran's proxy by destroying Hezbollah in Lebanon, Syria, and Iraq, thus weakening it.

Now it seems very clear. Russia has left Syria as well as Iran's military as the rebels took over. This sudden takeover was planned, funded, and organized by Turkey, which also plays a huge role in the end times.

This new power taking over Syria is much more radical; they are more of the ISIS types, camouflaged as moderate as its leader traded his terrorist outfit for a suit and tie to appease and fool the West.

Once the new leadership gets settled and the economy back on track with sanctions lifted by richer nations, they are capable of doing much more dramatic attacks on Israel than the Assad regime was willing to do. This new regime consists of religiously motived fanatics; Assad was more of a secular dictator. Time will tell.

As predicted in Isaiah 17, could it be that they launch a very destructive attack on Israel in the future, forcing Israel to destroy the entire city of Damascus never to be lived in again? Also to consider, Syria is not even mentioned in the Gog and Magog war as it is totally destroyed to the point that they are not really a nation anymore in the proper sense by that time.

Gog and Magog War

After a season of peace and prosperity, including new oil reserves discovered off the coast of Israel, another war is to take place. The Bible warns when there is peace and prosperity, watch out for sudden destruction and war.

In the war of Ezekiel 38, there is a whole new cast of characters and nations that are not bordering Israel. Those nearby nations are not even mentioned in this new war. The reason is that the previous war took care of the neighbors being destroyed and defeated to a point that they are no longer a threat. And most likely the Abraham Accords will have increased in participating nations including Saudi Arabia, causing great peace and prosperity within most of the Arab world and Israel.

The new nations that will form an alliance seem to be Iran, Russia, and Turkey as the main players, but other sub nations also align with them. For the first time in history, we are seeing Russia, Iran, and Turkey forming economic and military alliances. Once Israel wins this war—with God's help as the other nations do not come to Israel's aid as before—great rejoicing in the God of Israel will occur.

The USA and no other nation is mentioned as assisting Israel in this war. This time God alone helps them win, and it's so clear that it's God who helped Israel. This realization triggers a spiritual awaking and other events. But first the persecution of Jews in the diaspora (other nations) increases even more.

At the end of the Gog Magog War with Russia and Iran and other Muslim nations, harsh persecutions will immediately come against the Jews still living in the nations of the diaspora, most likely from Muslims living in those nations. For God also tells us in Ezekiel 39:25 (NKJV), "*Therefore thus says the Lord God, 'Now I will bring back the captives of Jacob, and have mercy on the whole house of Israel; and I will be jealous for My holy name....'*" This chapter 39 is referring to the time just after the Gog Magog war spoken of in Ezekiel 38.

Outpouring of Holy Spirit Revival: Right after war of Gog and Magog in Ezekiel 39:29 (NKJV) it says, "*'And I will not hide My face from them anymore; for I shall have poured out My Spirit on the house of Israel,' says the Lord God.*" This in turn triggers another great harvest of souls and spiritual awakening both in Israel and worldwide. In fact, many in Israel will become believers in Jesus/Yeshua after this great victory from the God of Israel! God will pour out His Spirit on Israel during this time.

But this also causes greater persecution of believers living inside Israel. Also the temple in Jerusalem will most likely be built during this time or before. The reason Israel can finally build their third temple is because the neighboring nations that would not allow it are so defeated they are no longer a threat to fear if a third temple is created. In fact, the rebuilding of this third temple is most likely accepted by the nations in the expanded Abraham Accords.

Of course, we know that when we see a temple built we know we are really in the end times, but the glory and power of God only increases as God always wins in the end! The Bible promises protection for the remnant who hear and obey Him to flee Jerusalem during this time.

Matthew 24:15-16 (NIV) says, *"So when you see standing in the holy place 'the abomination that causes desolation,' spoken of through the prophet Daniel—let the reader understand—then let those who are in Judea flee to the mountains."*

So the Bible gives us some clear signposts and key triggers that cause worldwide harvest and revival as well as the Second Coming of the Messiah being near.

The Joel End-Time Outpouring

Joel 2 is about the outpouring of the Holy Spirit. In fact in Acts 2 when the Holy Spirit fell on those there in the Upper Room, Peter quoted Joel 2:28-32 (NKJV):

> *And it shall come to pass afterward that I will pour out My Spirit on all flesh; your sons and your daughters*

> *shall prophesy, your old men shall dream dreams, your young men shall see visions. And also on My menservants and on My maidservants I will pour out My Spirit in those days. And I will show wonders in the heavens and in the earth: Blood and fire and pillars of smoke. The sun shall be turned into darkness, and the moon into blood, before the coming of the great and awesome day of the Lord. And it shall come to pass that whoever calls on the name of the Lord shall be saved. For in Mount Zion and in Jerusalem there shall be deliverance, as the Lord has said, Among the remnant whom the Lord calls.*

But he did not read the next few verses after Joel 2:32. Why is that? Could it be because those were reserved for our day. The last great outpouring of the Holy Spirit leading to the last great harvest of souls?

Peter ended his sermon in Acts 2:19-21 (NKJV) with:

> *I will show wonders in heaven above and signs in the earth beneath: blood and fire and vapor of smoke. The sun shall be turned into darkness, and the moon into blood, before the coming of the great and awesome day of the Lord. And it shall come to pass that whoever calls on the name of the Lord shall be saved.*

Peter did not read the next verse (Joel 3:1) possibly because it was not for his day, but for our day? Joel 3:1 (NKJV) reads: *"For behold, in those days and at that time, when I bring back the captives of Judah and Jerusalem,"* What does *"those days"* mean? It means possibly in our generation and lifetime or those days of those events! Why is that? Because God is bringing His people back to the land of Israel as it says in those days.

What day and what time is God referring to here? I think it's also in our day when there are more blood moons, outpourings of the Holy Spirit on men and women with prophetic and visions increasing like never before, and people calling on the name of the Lord to be saved as we see today. But the next verse gives an even better hint.

Joel 3:2 (KJV) tells us, *"I will also gather all nations, and will bring them down into the valley of Jehoshaphat, and will plead with them there for my people and for my heritage Israel, whom they have scattered among the nations, and parted my land."*

During Peter's time, Israel was not scattered, but they were living in their homeland under Roman occupation. They were not scattered at that point and there were no talks about a peace plan to partition Israel and give away places like Gaza, half of Jerusalem, or other areas. But this is occurring now in our modern times. But I believe that this also means that the great final outpouring of the Holy Spirit leading to the final harvest is also at hand in our day!

For any harvest you need great rain. We have the seeds of prayer, fasting, and past revivals—but we need a fresh rain to receive a fresh harvest! We can't expect the greatest harvest of souls by trying to live off renewals and revivals of the past. We need to encounter God in a fresh way as they did in the Upper Room, which led to a mass harvest of souls! Let's be refilled with the refreshing of the Holy Spirit and a fresh outpouring of the Spirit of revival and intimacy with Jesus.

CHAPTER 4

BECOMING UNKILLABLE

I believe we are living in the latter part of human history. In the last days, the Bible says there will be wars, diseases, sickness, and pestilence. (See Luke 21:11 NKJV.) It is inevitable. Do not wait until there is a plague or a nuclear disaster; prepare your body now. The wise foresee the evil and prepares. (See Proverbs 22:2-4 NKJV.)

John G. Lake, missionary and founder of Apostolic Faith Mission of South Africa in the early twentieth century, was passionate about health and healing the sick. He had a spiritual understanding of the science of health and how the law of health in Jesus Christ protects us. During his missionary work in South Africa, people were dying of the bubonic plague. The government sent supplies and a corps of doctors, but John G. Lake was praying for the sick with no personal protective equipment.

One of the doctors sent for him and asked him the secret to not getting infected. Lake's response and the ensuing conversation:

> "Brother that is the law of the Spirit of life in Christ Jesus," John replied. "I believe that just as long as I keep my soul in contact with the living God so that His Spirit is flowing into my soul and body, no germ will ever attach itself to me, for the Spirit of God will kill it."

> "Don't you think that you had better use our preventatives?" the doctor asked.
>
> "No, but doctor I think that you would like to experiment with me. If you will go over to one of these dead people and take the foam that comes out of their lungs after death and then put it under the microscope, you will see masses of living germs. You will find they are alive until a reasonable time after a man is dead. You can fill my hand with them and I will keep it under the microscope, and instead of these germs remaining alive, they will die instantly."
>
> They tried it and just as John said, the germs died on contact with him. The doctor was astonished.
>
> "What is that?" he asked.
>
> "That is the law of the Spirit of life in Christ Jesus. When a man's spirit and a man's body are filled with the blessed presence of God, it oozes out of the pores of your flesh and kills the germs. Suppose on the other hand, my soul had been under the law of death, and I were in fear and darkness? The very opposite would have been the result. The result would have been that my body would have absorbed the germs, these would have generated disease and I would have died."[5]

Psalm 91:7-8 (NKJV) says, "*A thousand may fall at your side, ten thousand at your right hand; but it shall not come near you. Only with your eyes shall you look, and see the reward of the wicked.*" Quoting this Scripture is not enough. You must fill your body and spirit with life and the presence of God. When the black plague hit Europe in the 1340s, it annihilated half of the population, but Jews were not being affected in the same way as others. Accusations started to fly that they were responsible for the disease. But in reality, it was the Jewish laws of cleanliness and dietary restrictions that caused the immunity along with the Lord's protection. They followed the diet given to them by God, so their bodies were saturated with life, enabling them to resist the disease.

Sickness, disease, and pestilence are inevitable, but how cool would it be if you are able to resist ill health? I reiterate—if you were able to preempt illness. Often people get sick as the season changes to winter, or to spring as the body is trying to remove the past season's toxics as it goes into the new season, similar to spring cleaning your home. Apart from prayer you can also remove the previous season's toxins out of your body by going on a fast, a three-day juice cleanse, or colonics. You can start small, maybe once a year, but I encourage you to do something.

An effective way to cleanse is to drink juice in the morning. The juice acts as liquid energy. Initially, you might get hungry before it is time for your next meal, so have a smoothie or shake for lunch. Smoothies are thicker, and as you add more healthy ingredients to the blender, you will feel fuller throughout the day. You may feel weak, hungry, or headachy for the first three days because your body is craving the old fleshly nature, but these symptoms will subside or be less severe by the fourth day. If you are concerned about feeling hungry, add avocado to your smoothie. That should satisfy you until dinner.

How would you like to raise the dead? How would you like to see mass resurrections? It is possible when you have the power of God, the faith of God, and the health of God to not only see healing, but to keep you clean and healthy in the event of the inevitable. You will be one of the ones whose hair is not falling out or dying from radiation poisoning. What a supernatural witness that would be—so full of health that your body just zaps sickness. How would you like to have that kind of witness?

There have been times when I just walked by people and they got healed, just like Peter's shadow in Acts 5:15. This can happen when your spirit, body, emotions, and mind are in sync with Heaven. When your thoughts are in sync with Heaven, you think of your destiny, you think the best of others and on things that are lovely and of good report. When your emotions are in sync with a sound mind, you love everybody, you forgive everybody, and you are not easily offended. Reading and declaring God's Word, praying, and worshipping strengthens your spirit, which all affects your physical body. When every area of your life is on a high, it sparks breakthrough. Everything must come together synergistically.

A prime natural example of synergy is the famous golfer, Tiger Woods. He dominated professional golf in the late 1990s. But did you notice when his personal life spiraled out of control, his career tanked? He was emotionally out of sync. Even though he had the expertise and the physical training, he was emotionally depleted. The stress of losing his family, the guilt, shame, and loneliness took its toll on him, affecting his physical performance. It took him a couple of years to make a comeback because, again, one thing affects the other.

Famous actors, with seemingly everything going for them suddenly commit suicide. Why? Because they had money and fame, but they were spiritually and emotionally bankrupt.

When the devil tempted Jesus in the wilderness, Jesus knew the enemy had no hold on Him. Jesus had no hooks. He had nothing for the devil to pull Him with. His mind, body, spirit, and emotions were in sync with each other and with Heaven. If you have a hook, you can guarantee the devil will use it.

Let us say you do everything else right. You are loving people, you are living your destiny, and just an all-around good person, but your eating habits are terrible—the devil has a hook. He goes about like a roaring lion, seeking whom he may devour (1 Peter 5:8). He is our accuser, always looking for ways to destroy our life and derail our destiny. The evil one says, "Since they aren't eating healthy or following God's dietary laws, their body is a perfect environment for cancer to grow." The enemy attacks people with cancer, but they may have opened the door for him to waltz right in.

I'm not judging, and this is not always the case, but many times sicknesses can be directly related to an unhealthy and sedentary lifestyle—inadequate rest, copious amounts of soda, sugary foods, unhealthy carbs in excess, and other poor lifestyle choices. All of these combined have been proven by doctors and science to create a cancerous state over time.

Unkillable

The apostle Paul was put in prison, escaped murder at the hands of Jewish leaders, was shipwrecked, stoned, and was even bitten by a deadly serpent, and yet, he survived it all. John was boiled alive in oil and came out unscathed. Paul and John were unkillable until God said it was their time. In the last days, I believe some people will be unkillable; or if they are killed, they will resurrect, like Lazarus and the two witnesses. Some will not be killed unless God allows it.

"*Whoever eats My flesh and drinks My blood has eternal life, and I will raise him up at the last day*" (John 6:54 NKJV). This Scripture refers to spiritual death, but I believe it has physical implications as well.

When you partake of the power of the blood and body of Jesus, the same power that raised Him from the dead starts to flow through you to re-create cells in your body, killing sick cells, and resurrecting your organs. I believe the blood of Jesus can and will extend your life. Then you only die if God allows it or its your time, but not prematurely as many do because of their life choices and without realizing that it contributes to leaving this earth early.

In France, there is a statue of Saint Denis holding his decapitated head at the Saint Denis Subway Station right outside of Paris. He lost his head to the guillotine for preaching the raw gospel of God. Story has it that they cut his head off, and he picked it up and walked back to his executioners with his head in his hand. They have a celebration every year and the Saint Denis parade in his honor. So, the same people who killed him now celebrate him. Interesting, is it not? Guess what. It really happened. This is a true story. Do you believe it is possible?

The apostle John was boiled in the hottest oil and he did not die. This was supposed to be an execution, but John did not even feel the effects of the boiling-hot oil and water. It was just as Daniel in the lions' den emerged unharmed and the three Hebrew children who went into the hottest flames didn't fall dead, even though the heat killed the guards standing nearby.

There is a dimension of the glory that we can become unkillable if we are in His will and living His way in the destiny God has for us until the timing of the Lord allows it.

Paul was in prison writing, no contemplating, whether it was better for him to go be with the Lord in martyrdom or to stay behind awhile longer to help the new church grow. In Philippians 1:23-24 (AMPC) he tells us:

> *But I am hard pressed between the two. My yearning desire is to depart (to be free of this world, to set forth) and be with Christ, for that is far, far better; but to remain in my body is more needful and essential for your sake.*

It's as if Paul had the choice presented to him to be taken to Heaven or continue awhile longer on earth. How would you like to have such a relationship with the Lord that He gives you the option and trusts you to decide whether to stay or go to Heaven? It's as if he told the jailers and the rulers of that day, "Me and God are having a meeting about my fate, I'll let you know what we decide; until then, could you bring me another pen and more paper." There was no fear of death. It seemed to have been a choice between God and Paul at that point.

Characters like Enoch literally just left this earth and never experienced death, though that has not been the norm. I believe there is a remnant who will be unkillable in the last days until His return. This does not mean some are not called to be martyrs and that is a precious, high prize in the Lord's eyes. There are different callings and endings, but it also takes faith to be one of those the enemy cannot take out before your time.

Pray to Be Counted Worthy to Escape What Is Coming

Luke 21:36 (NKJV) says, "*Watch therefore, and pray always that you may be counted worthy to escape all these things that will come to pass, and to stand before the Son of Man.*"

We know that the devil will try to kill as many people as he can on planet Earth before the Lord returns, before they can be saved. That's why we are in a race against time to save as many souls as possible. The enemy would love to kill as many of God's people as possible so they don't finish their assignment and expand His Kingdom, which diminishes satan's kingdom. He tries to do this through sickness, plagues, wars, unhealthy lifestyles, persecution, etc.

But I truly believe there is a level of the Glory of God combined with a fresh revelation on the blood of Jesus that when fully activated can make a believer unkillable, unless of course with permission from the Lord and it's that person's time to go. Even Job was not allowed to be killed by satan himself. That is exciting news! You can be set free from the fear and sting of death!

What would you do for the Lord if you had no fear of death! We have gone to many nations that in the natural are known to be highly dangerous and also into areas where there has been war. I've even been in Israel seeing missiles explode right above my head and literally in front of our hotel, but they were extinguished by the Iron Dome and lots of angels. The funny thing is we feel absolutely zero fear even when the sirens go off and we have to run to a bomb shelter; it's just a requirement, but the joy of the Lord is with us always.

Communion Revelation

Then there is the whole revelation on Communion. Talk about healthy food—there is power in the blood of Jesus! Symbolically partaking of the blood and body of Jesus through Communion changes your DNA. I do agree that you should not take Communion if you are struggling with some type of sin that you don't want to let go of, unless of course you are ready to let it go. I know people who have been instantly healed and set free from sin and addictions during a Communion service. His blood and body were shed and broken for your healing, deliverance, peace, prosperity, dominion, and authority. If you want to be delivered, you should take Communion.

Are you willing to fill your mind and body with God's presence, His glory, and His Word? He saved you. Your body and your mind are not your own. You do not get to do what you want with it. You are only borrowing it for the years you are on earth. Your body is the temple of God. Make it hard for the devil to kill you. It is time to clean the junk and the idols out. Idols? Yes, addictions, including food addictions, are idols. Get free from them and replenish your body. It will thank you with more energy, a better outlook, and an overall good feeling.

5

DNA BLOOD RESET

Before I formed you in the womb I knew you, before you were born I set you apart; I appointed you as a prophet to the nations

(Jeremiah 1:5 NIV).

God is a Spirit (John 4:24), and He breathed "spirit" into Adam and Eve (Genesis 2:7). You also are spirit put in a human body. The spirit part of you is from the eternal heavenly realm. Your spirit that God created will always exist, even though your body will fade away.

For those God foreknew he also predestined to be conformed to the likeness of his Son, that he might be the firstborn among many brothers and sisters. And those he predestined, he also called; those he called, he also justified; those he justified, he also glorified (Romans 8:29-30 NIV).

Then when you were conceived and formed in your mother's womb, you had two destinies pulling at you. On the one hand you had the destiny that God put into you, and on the other hand you had the destiny of sin—that which all humans have been born into once we were conceived in the womb due to the fall of Adam and Eve and all your ancestors before you (Romans 5:12).

Then one day you received Jesus as your Lord and Savior and received salvation, and your spirit began to be alive again unto God (Romans 6:11). As you once again started to *know* God and commune with Him, you began to get hints of His destiny and calling for you. Maybe you even get prophetic words confirming what you felt deep down inside God was calling you to. Then you might even have noticed your talents and gifts that fit in with the calling of God. Finally you start to see what God had preplanned all along.

> *For we are God's handiwork, created in Christ Jesus to do good works, which God prepared in advance for us to do* (Ephesians 2:10 NIV).

New DNA

God has a destiny that He has already created for you. And He is waiting for you to walk into it once you know and see what that calling is. The problem many people encounter is finding out exactly what that full calling and destiny is. There are forces at work that cloud our sight from seeing fully what that calling and destiny is. Once we see it clearly, things start to change.

We are saved and receive eternal life when we are born again. The problem is that most Christians, even though they are born again, still get pulled in two directions. When they are in the spirit, they are really after the things of God; but often other forces also pull them in other directions.

In each of our bloodlines we have relatives, parents, and (further up the chain) ancestors who had sins and also gifts and callings, which get carried down to us. Yes, you are saved; but more often than not, you realize you still have to crucify the flesh and stay in the spirit. When you are pulled in the wrong direction, often it is in directions that the enemy knows are your weaknesses due to your bloodline. It's one thing to ask God to forgive you of sin, but it's quite another to get that pattern of sin broken off you and your family line.

Even though King David's sin with Bathsheba was forgiven (2 Samuel 11; 12:1-13), we see the consequences of the sexual sin being carried down the bloodline to his sons, including King Solomon's desire for many women/wives. Solomon, who had traits in his DNA from his father King David, had the callings of kingship, worship, etc., but he was also pulled in the direction of lust for many women. He even went one step further to not only marry pagan women but to worship their gods, which led to his demise.

This pulling in different directions is why often you can see people growing in the gifts and callings as they are faithful to pray and nurture the gifts; yet all the while, they never deal with the sin pattern in their DNA passed down to them. Then one day they reach a very high place in God or in their ministry or business only to have a terrible fall that affects many people. Many wonder how this could be or if they were ever really close to God. The reality is that the wheat often grows with the tares; but the tares get so big, if not cut off, they choke out the wheat and all the good that was done. They were being pulled in both directions.

Often the success of the blessing of increase of gifts and callings causes people to let their guard down. They get so busy in their callings that they start to slow down their times of intimacy with God, which allows the sin nature to increase and take over.

Many people are able to keep their sins at bay and not let them rule them or destroy them, but they never really totally allow God to destroy and kill the pattern of sin. This is often due to lack of understanding of how this all works or else they go into denial.

Paul also dealt with this as he wrote in Romans 7:15 (NKJV): *"For what I am doing, I do not understand. For what I will to do, that I do not practice; but what I hate, that I do."* Paul continues talking about the struggle of the two destinies in our bloodline fighting for dominance when he writes in Romans 7:20-25 (NIV):

> *Now if I do what I do not want to do, it is no longer I who do it, but it is sin living in me that does it. So I find this law at work: Although I want to do good, evil is right there with me. For in my inner being I delight in God's law; but I see another law at work in me, waging war against the law of my mind and making me a prisoner of the law of sin at work within me. What a wretched man I am! Who will rescue me from this body that is subject to death? Thanks be to God, who delivers me through Jesus Christ our Lord! So then, I myself in my mind am a slave to God's law, but in my sinful nature a slave to the law of sin.*

The Blood

In our blood is our DNA. Our DNA is like a scroll or a book. If you could open your book of your destiny encoded in your

DNA, you could see your future callings as well as past sins of your family line; these are also encoded in your DNA. In a sense, your DNA programs you toward a certain destiny. The only thing that can change the program is to cleanse and change the DNA through the blood of Jesus and allow His life to consume every part of your life.

Today scientists and doctors claim they can re-create body parts with just DNA strands because the DNA has the source code embedded in it to re-create the entire body.

Most people understand DNA to have two strands intertwined. But that is what humans can see. There is an invisible third strand that surrounds our DNA called RNA. This invisible strand is the spirit part of our DNA that is connected to our physical DNA that scientists cannot see. In it is contained the spiritual blueprint of our destiny and calling. It is connected and part of the other two strands. We are both physical and spirit beings, and our spirit is interconnected to our physical and intellectual nature—and God has welded it all together.

The Bible says that in Christ Jesus we are new creatures (2 Corinthians 5:17 KJV). God can reprogram and change your DNA. He does this through the perfect undefiled untainted blood of Jesus. When you partake of the blood of Jesus by faith and it comes into you, it has the power to break off every sinful pattern in your generational line. But it has to be accessed on purpose.

Just having a right to it is not the same as actually activating the power of the blood of Jesus.

When you take Communion, you can activate the DNA of God through Jesus into your DNA. Something supernatural happens when you take the blood and body of Jesus at Communion. Life is in the blood (Leviticus 17:11). When you take communion you can actually reactivate the power of His blood every time you take it by faith, taking on His life which is in His blood.

> *Then Jesus said to them, "Most assuredly, I say to you, unless you eat the flesh of the Son of Man and drink His blood, you have no life in you. Whoever eats My flesh and drinks My blood has eternal life, and I will raise him up at the last day"* (John 6:53-54 NKJV).

God always works by covenant. He always keeps His end of the covenant. When you take Communion, which represents Jesus' blood and body, it activates the covenant, thus activating the DNA of God's life into yours.

> *While they were eating, Jesus took bread, and when he had given thanks, he broke it, and gave it to his disciples, saying, "Take and eat; this is my body." Then he took a cup, and when he had given thanks, he gave it to them, saying, "Drink from it, all of you. This is my blood of the covenant, which is poured out for many for the forgiveness of sins"* (Matthew 26:26-28 NIV).

The blood of His covenant seems to have been a lost message in our day. We don't hear teachings much anymore on the power of the blood or songs about it as there used to be. The truth is that the devil knows all too well that when we get ahold of the revelation of the blood and how to activate the blood of Jesus into our DNA, our entire life—body, spirit, and abilities—starts to shift to a higher plane! That is why the devil uses blood sacrifice in satanic rituals and in many secret societies as it activates a demonic power. When we have the original power of God's covenant, how much less the enemy can only try to copy with a much inferior sacrifice.

We have seen people healed and delivered many times while partaking of Communion, when it is done with revelation and faith as opposed to doing it just out of habit. Faith and revelation are the needed ingredients.

Because you are a son or daughter of God, you have His DNA! The more you conform to His image and allow Him to change you, the more you will become like Him (Romans 8:29). Your DNA can actually be altered when you allow the DNA of God into you. Not only will your body start to be transformed as sick cells suddenly start to be healed and regenerated, but the RNA spirit strand of your DNA will be reactivated and suddenly you start to tap back into your original call and destiny.

Even dormant gifts, talents, and abilities can start to surface that you never even knew you had. People lost in drug addiction have been radically saved and Spirit-filled and changed, only to later discover they had dormant business, leadership, or other skills or spiritual gifts that started to surface once they allowed the blood of Jesus to do its total work. When you allow the power of the blood to break every curse on your DNA, it makes room for the redemptive gifts and callings to surface once all the weeds are gone.

Many believers stop at salvation and never let God do the complete work of crucifying their sinful nature and desires that are programmed into their DNA. God's complete work activates their full destiny so they can see the fullness of what God has for them. That is why Paul writes in Hebrews:

> *Therefore, since we are surrounded by such a huge crowd of witnesses to the life of faith, let us strip off every weight that slows us down, especially the sin that*

> *so easily trips us up. And let us run with endurance the race God has set before us* (Hebrews 12:1 NLT).

When we allow God to totally break and crucify the sinful nature within us, it activates the supernatural side of our DNA. The weight we need to lay aside, which often slows us down from reaching our peak in God, is the sinful nature embedded in our DNA.

God wants to take you from just *saved* to *totally transformed* into His image—body, soul, and spirit—to fulfill the full destiny and calling on your life.

> *The sinful nature wants to do evil, which is just the opposite of what the Spirit wants. And the Spirit gives us desires that are the opposite of what the sinful nature desires. These two forces are constantly fighting each other, so you are not free to carry out your good intentions* (Galatians 5:17 NLT).

When you live in the Spirit, filling your thoughts and life with the Kingdom of Heaven and allowing His Spirit in you to dominate, it starts to weaken and destroy the desires and works of the flesh in your life. Yes, you are technically the righteousness of God in Christ Jesus (2 Corinthians 5:21), but you still need to activate it. Just like you are healed by His stripes and God provided for all your needs on the Cross, you need to activate it by faith to get it to manifest in your life.

After the reopening of a sin or pattern of sin, ask God not just to forgive you of sins or sinful desires that spring up, but ask Him to break them off completely through His blood, to live a crucified life, and to be continually filled with His Spirit. Then allow Him to fully activate His DNA in you!

> *Therefore, dear brothers and sisters you have no obligation to do what your sinful nature urges you to do. For if you live by its dictates, you will die. But if through the power of the Spirit you put to death the deeds of your sinful nature, you will live. For all who are led by the Spirit of God are children of God* (Romans 8:12-14 NLT).

Resurrection Power

Through Jesus' DNA living in you, you can activate the power of His resurrection. *"And if the Spirit of him who raised Jesus from the dead is living in you, he who raised Christ from the dead will also give life to your mortal bodies because of his Spirit who lives in you"* (Romans 8:11 NIV). In His Word it is written that God can give resurrection life to our mortal bodies as well as our spirit! Imagine, every time you get sick in your body you can activate the power that raised Christ from the dead!

One of the ways to activate this is through taking Communion with revelation. When you allow the blood and body of Jesus by faith to activate His life and DNA and resurrection in you, good things start to happen. In fact, Jesus says that those who eat His flesh and drink His blood will never die:

> *Yes, I am the bread of life! Your ancestors ate manna in the wilderness, but they all died. Anyone who eats the bread from heaven, however, will never die* (John 6:48-50 NLT).

Of course, we know this is referring to eternal life, but in Romans 8:11, it also says we can experience the same resurrection power and life in our mortal bodies!

I believe there will be people on earth in the last days who will literally be "unkillable" due to this revelation being activated. Some will get resurrected if they are killed. In the book of Revelation, it talks about the two witnesses being killed but then resurrecting (Revelation 11:3-12).

John was supposed to be boiled to death, and they could not kill him. So they stuck him on an island to die of starvation and thirst. That did not work either. He wrote the book of Revelation while he was on that Isle of Patmos. He just would not die until God said it was time.

Paul was stoned. Later he walked away from the stoning only to preach in the next city (Acts 14:19-20). No one was supposed to get up after a stoning, it was a death sentence. The person was to be stoned to death. I believe that Paul most likely was actually stoned to death and died and most likely resurrected, as I'm sure the people stoning him knew how to determine if Paul was dead and to keep battering him with rocks until he died. He seemed to be unkillable between the shipwreck, stoning, and a venous serpent bite—he just would not die until it was his time.

In fact, Paul wrote that he was contemplating whether it was better for him to go now and be with Jesus or stay back for the church's sake. He was close enough to God to have a discussion on the terms of his departure from this world. How would you like to have that type of relationship with Jesus? That even your death is not a mystery and you could discuss it with the Lord and come to an agreement on it.

Paul writes in Philippians 1:23-24 (NLT): *"I'm torn between two desires: I long to go and be with Christ, which would be far better for me. But for your sakes, it is better that I continue to live."*

Hezekiah was able to have that discussion, and God extended his life by 15 years.

Daniel did not die in the lions' den, a death sentence he had been given (Daniel 6:16-23). Daniel's three friends were sentenced to death in the fiery furnace that burned so hot it killed the guards outside the furnace. Yet the three were untouched by the fire, as a fourth Being was with them in the furnace (Daniel 3:15-27). Many believe the fourth was an epiphany, Jesus appearing.

God can so invigorate you with His DNA and resurrection power flowing in you that you can become unstoppable to anything the enemy throws at you, unless God calls you home. Some who normally should have died may have extremely longer life spans, and others will live until the Second Coming of the Lord as "*those that are alive and remain....*"

6

END-TIME ANGELS

Angels will be greatly used in the end times.

I had a glimpse of these end-time angels during a crusade I was preaching in Mexico City, Mexico. We had more than 22,000 people in the indoor stadium and the highest level of the Glory of God ripped through the stadium. Masses of souls were saved and some of the most amazing, notable, and creative miracles occurred.

During the worship my spiritual eyes were opened and I could see extremely large angel beings that looked more like soldiers with very serious expressions, not to be messed with. They were activated when major harvests occurred!

Cindy Jacobs also spoke at this crusade, and she saw the angel over Mexico. As she was describing it while onstage, the power of God ripped through the stadium and she herself could barely stand up. Later in the green room with Cindy and Mike, suddenly the glory and power of God ripped through the room and we found ourselves, along with the staff, helpers, and even kids, weeping and interceding on the floor with groans of intercession. Heaven just suddenly stepped into the green room. I believe the archangel over Mexico had released the burden for that nation and key city at that time. That angel also was somehow used in the mass harvest of souls that we were seeing!

Angels are key to this present move of God. When you operate in Heaven's glory, being aware of the angelic is key. Most people are not aware of angels and their functions and how much they can help us. I have noticed that when you acknowledge the presence of angels, they increase; and when you release them to work on your behalf, they do amazing things. I've discovered that the more I welcome and acknowledge the presence of angels, the more powerful demonstrations of Heaven begin to happen in and outside of my meetings.

Some people purposely ignore angels with the idea that they don't want to give them too much credit for fear they might give them too much praise. But often the same people will overly focus on the demonic realm, knowing the names of every demon and principality but not have a clue about the angelic realm that can counter every demon.

For example, there are *territorial angels*. When you enter a region and allow the angel assigned to that territory to be released and move with you, amazing things happen in those regions. Most Christians will spend years binding up "territorial spirits," but never even bother to ask what angel is the main angel that God had assigned to that territory. Remember, the enemy is a copycat who copies God; he cannot create. He copies the structure and order of how God does things. God has archangels over regions, so the devil puts in *principalities*.

> *For we do not wrestle against flesh and blood, but against* ***principalities****, against powers, against the rulers of the darkness of this age, against spiritual hosts of wickedness in the heavenly places* (Ephesians 6:12 NKJV).

Then there are lower-level demons under the principalities, which is a copy of angels working under the archangels, and so forth.

Once you start to operate from Heaven's governmental structure as opposed to starting off only binding the enemy's copy of God's structure, you can start to see some real change occur in cities and regions. Even if you were to successfully chase out a demonic principality without understanding the angels that are to fill that vacuum in that region, it will just come back stronger.

One day I was preaching in a crusade in Africa. The first night I had a very hard time. There simply was no breakthrough. It was an area inundated and known as a center for witchcraft and Freemasonry, and the meeting was right next to a cemetery. My host told me after the first night that even Reinhard Bonnke was very frustrated when he had come there to preach.

The next day I went into a much higher glory realm. I also praised and worshipped all day along with more fasting, and I asked hundreds of other intercessors to press in. I also asked the angels of Heaven for major backup. When I showed up the next night, the atmosphere was electric. As I took the stage, I felt led to continue singing creative prophetic songs, as the worship team backed me up. Suddenly a demonized woman I called "Catwoman" approached the stage. She was hissing like a cat and making a sign like she wanted to scratch me.

Amazingly, none of the ushers would stop her. I had two options. The knee-jerk reaction of most believers would be to start commanding the demon to go. That would have been fine, but I did not want the focus of the meeting to go from worshipping in the glory with tens of thousands, to focusing on a demon that wanted attention.

The Lord told me I had another more powerful option—keep worshipping and employ the help of angels. As I led the people in spontaneous worship, I could see and sense thousands of angels. The Lord told me to point out where I saw them, and I did just that. Where I would point, suddenly thousands of people would go down in the spirit and experience mass deliverances, foaming at the mouth, and screaming as demons fled in mass. The difference with option two was that I allowed the angels to assist in the deliverances as opposed to only me doing all the work one by one.

It was a glorious night as thousands were set free and many came running for salvation, even those who were far from the meeting but could hear the screams. They ran to see what was happening and ended up getting saved also. "Catwoman," as I called her at the time, received a massive deliverance, as I simply asked the angels on my right and left to help the woman. She fell out kicking and screaming, and then she was in total peace and in her right mind. We even had a resurrection that very weekend. It went from a not-so-good result to above and beyond what I could ask or think simply by inviting Heaven and the angelic to participate in the meeting.

Most believers' angels are so bored, possibly taking up knitting, because they never release them and work together with them to see the Kingdom of God advance. Throughout the Bible angels are ever present, working with the saints to advance the Kingdom of God.

First of all, Jesus gets all the glory for anything that angels do, as they are servants of God. When you see a car swerve into your lane and you cry out, "Jesus," or "God, help me," and at the very last second somehow the car didn't crash into your car, let me explain what happens. We ask the Father in the name of

Jesus, then God uses the Holy Spirit who is on earth, and the Holy Spirit releases angels to actually do the job of protecting you.

The enemy follows, or I should say copies, Heaven's ways and structure but in the demonic realm. People in satanism and witchcraft will speak in the name of Lucifer or his other names, but the devil himself does not do the work but releases demons that are on earth to afflict people, etc.

Once you know and understand how the heavenly structure operates, you can effectively operate to see changes *"on earth as it is in heaven"* (Matthew 6:10).

Types of Angels

This exciting section and the following seven sections are taken from my book, *The Courts of Heaven,* Chapter 3, "Angels." There are amazingly different types of angels and heavenly beings. Not all are angels, as the Bible mentions both angels and heavenly hosts in the same passage but as two different beings (Luke 2:13). There are living creatures, living lights, and so many more. But for simplicity in this chapter, I refer to most of them as angels.

There are *healing angels* that speed up the healing power. There are angels that assist in miraculously protecting you from car accidents and injury, as I'm sure you have had some close calls that you attribute to the protection of God. When I travel and speak, people often report seeing at least two huge angels on my right and left that many say are as big as 30 feet tall. Several seers have confirmed telling me that they can only see up to their knees most times, as they go right through the ceiling.

One time at a regional meeting in Dallas, I saw the huge angel standing nearby, and I asked people who were sick to stand right in the exact spot where the angel stood. Every person who walked up near the spot was struck down to the floor very fast and stood up totally healed. This included a man who had broken his neck in many places. He was a backslidden healing evangelist from the 1960s and '70s who gave his life back to God that night.

Another time I was in Israel, in the Golan Heights near the border of Syria, conducting meetings. The Hebrew/Russian translator kept getting knocked out in the spirit. So they got another translator, and the second translator had the same experience. Great joy and healings occurred that night in Israel. These huge angels I like to call "Mighty Ones" are like major bodyguards but seem to also assist in healing, deliverance, etc.

I can better understand after these experiences what Elisha felt when surrounded and outnumbered by the Syrian army. It was just him and his servant, who was basically freaking out thinking he was about to die. Elisha could see entire armies of angels ready to protect them. Elisha prayed that his servant's eyes would be opened to see the angelic armies, and God opened his eyes (2 Kings 6:15-17). Once Elisha's servant's eyes were opened, they were both in faith, which also helped to activate the angels on their behalf. This is where faith and glory intersect. I, too, pray that God opens your spiritual eyes and senses to see or discern the presence of angels in your midst.

As mentioned previously, there are *territorial angels*. These angels help take your city for the Lord. They are the "earth or land angels." Whenever I fly back home and drive into town, every single time I am at the city limits I can feel the territorial angels welcoming me as I arrive. A wave of the presence of God bouncing off these angels enters my car and greets me. They are assigned to your territory.

Life is so much easier when you work with these angels, as they can do much of the "heavy lifting."

Healing, miracle, and signs and wonders angels are also interesting. Many times when I am in very hard areas of unreached people groups—Muslims, Jewish people, New Age people, government officials, or others—and need God to validate the message, I ask God to release these angels; and they are more than willing. Signs and wonders, healings, and miracles will occur, validating the message of the gospel with a harvest of souls following.

Don't depend only on your personal gifts God gave you and your own faith, but tap into Heaven's faith and arsenal and you will see God do things often beyond your own giftings and personal faith. Use your faith to get into the glory realm and to release angels so that much more can be accomplished.

Angels of Supernatural Transportation

Several times I have been supernaturally transported from one city and even from one nation to another while driving, arriving at my destination miraculously fast. One time an eight-hour drive across France became a two-hour drive, as we started to worship and the angelic stepped in allowing us to make the meeting in time. Another time in New Zealand a one-hour drive was hampered by a flock of sheep blocking our way. When they finally passed we were so late, but we asked God for supernatural transportation and we were there somehow in 15 minutes.

Elijah experienced these types of things and would often be transported, causing others to search for him.

> *As surely as the Lord your God lives, there is not a nation or kingdom where my master has not sent someone to look for you. And whenever a nation or kingdom claimed you were not there, he made them swear they could not find you. But now you tell me to go to my master and say, "Elijah is here." I don't know where the Spirit of the Lord may carry you when I leave you. If I go and tell Ahab and he doesn't find you, he will kill me"* (1 Kings 18:10-12 NIV).

Being supernaturally transported was common with Elijah. On the day Elijah departed into Heaven, they searched three days for him, which could indicate that was how long it took to find him every time he was transported (2 Kings 2:17). Elijah's final transportation to Heaven was via angelic chariot (2 Kings 2:11). Angels can take you not just to Heaven but back and forth on earth. We could talk about Philip being transported (Acts 8:39) and so on.

According to the Acts of the Apostles, after Philip baptized the Ethiopian eunuch, he was "caught away" by the Spirit and "found at Azotus" (Ashdod), and then *"passing through he preached in all the cities till he came to Caesarea"* (Acts 8:40).

Now we know the Holy Spirit is on earth helping us in many ways, and one of these ways can be supernatural transportation when God deems it necessary. When the Holy Spirit is moving and doing a work, angels are part of the process in some way as angels are here on earth to assist believers.

Hebrews 1:14 (NIV) tells us, *"Are not all angels ministering spirits sent to serve those who will inherit salvation?"*

In John 6:16-21 (NIV), when Jesus got into the boat after He walked on the water, "*immediately the boat reached the shore where they were heading*" (verse 21). It could also mean "very quickly." Whatever the case, after Jesus got into the boat, it either was teleported to the shore or was in some other way brought to shore very rapidly. Either way, this amazing miracle is often overlooked, so it does not surprise me that this often happens driving to an event to minister.

So we know that being transported is clearly in the Bible in the Old and New Testament. Also it's clear that it's a work of the "Spirit," which would refer to the Holy Spirit on earth. The Holy Spirit on earth also works with ministering spirits or angels to assist God's people. I expect we will see more and more of these types of supernatural transportation in the days ahead as the gospel will be even more urgently needed in places that might not be easy to access or to avoid hindrances when traveling to share the gospel in time.

Angel of Time

The *angel of time* can take you back and forth through time; sometimes in your sleep, prayers, or other. I know of people who had dreams about ministering in nations, such as in the bush in Africa and in China. They later were invited there; so they went, taking the dream as a confirmation. When they arrived, the people thanked them for coming the second time, documenting the exact day of the dream. But for the people, they were really there.

Since God lives outside of time and angels can go back and forth from earth to Heaven and Heaven to earth outside of time, as in Jacob's ladder, they can also take you there too in the spirit, a vision, or other ways.

Angels of Provision

I have had many financial miracles and seen many for other people occur in our meetings. Angels can supernaturally be released to bring finances in time of need or things that are needed on time.

Of course, that does not negate sowing and reaping, which are all part of the provision of God. But angels can often be the messengers that bring the financial breakthrough. As you are faithful in your finances but still need the breakthrough, you can release angels to speed up the process.

Often the enemy tries to block the release of provision to God's people, especially when they are using it to advance the Kingdom of God, which is destroying the enemy's kingdom. It's like angels working for Brinks assigned to bring provision to you in armored vehicles so the enemy does not steal it on the way, which often occurs to many people unaware of the reason.

In the Bible, angels are depicted as bringing provision to people in need. One example is when an angel provided food and water to Elijah during his flight from Jezebel in 1 Kings 19. Another instance is when angels came to Sodom in the evening, and Lot, who was sitting at the gate of Sodom, saw them and rose to meet them (Genesis 19:1). Additionally, the Bible mentions that believers should not forget to show hospitality to strangers, as some have unknowingly hosted angels (Hebrews 13:2). These passages illustrate the role of angels in providing for those in need.

Legions of Angels

Legions of angels are armies of angels similar to what Elisha had access to. We also have the right to at least a legion of angels. On the Cross Jesus had the option to call on legions of angels to keep Him from being crucified on the Cross (Matthew 26:53). Of course, Jesus chose to stay so we could be saved. But the point is that He had access to legions of angels. Jesus says that *"all the power"* He has, has been given to us (Luke 10:19). That means if He had access to legions of angels while He walked the earth and He is our example, then we also have them at our disposal.

Often we perish in many areas for lack of knowledge. Once you know you have access and a right to something, you start to have faith to activate it. Once I realized the immense heavenly army I had at my disposal, I have kept my angels busy ever since. I just wish I had this revelation when I first started ministry over 20 years ago.

Angels Over Creation

There are angels assigned to the oceans, mountains, deserts, etc. There are also angels over wind, rain, snow, lightning, and thunder that all come out of the treasuries of Heaven. The enemy also tries to manipulate the weather patterns that God put over creation. When that occurred with Jesus on the boat on the Galilee, He spoke with authority and commanded the wind and waves to be still (Luke 8:24). The creation obeyed Jesus over the enemy once He spoke. In our day sometimes the weather is an attack or even man-made weather devices used to bring havoc. We have authority over the weather, and we have angels to back up God's words we speak under His direction and prompting.

When I was in Trinidad, I believe a very powerful angel was with me. Before I went on the trip, I told all my intercessors to pray that God would shake the island of Trinidad for His glory, as I was instructed by the Holy Spirit. Little did I realize how literal this would be. As we arrived and walked off the plane to fill out our customs paperwork, suddenly a 7.2 earthquake shook the entire airport and city. It was felt as far away as Jamaica. We saw the earth move like a snake and the rafters all were shaking. I discovered that the moment we set foot on the ground in Trinidad, buildings that housed financial centers involved in high-level corruption with the oil industry and the government were shaken and some destroyed.

Then we held revival meetings and many were very open to the message, receiving healing and salvation. A similar incident occurred in Oklahoma City, Oklahoma, as I was speaking on earthquakes in various places. My bed shook several times, such that I thought it might have been a tornado. Later I was told that up to that time earthquakes were not common in that part of Oklahoma. They were highlighting the message I was speaking.

Angels Even in Outer Space?

Hebrew's 1:14 (NIV) says, "*Are not all angels ministering spirits sent to serve those who will inherit salvation?*"

We know that the protection of the territory of Israel has been assigned to the archangel Michael. I believe every nation and territory has angels assigned to it as Israel is the prototype example for all nations. As Daniel fasted 21 days, this allowed the archangel to break through past the principality of the prince of Persia and visit Daniel with the message from the Lord. What if humans go to outer space?

One time, Russian cosmonauts encountered these angels, and it changed their lives. They reported back to their superiors in the USSR (as it was called at the time), and the government thought they had gone crazy since they were communist atheists and taught to believe there is no God. The Russian cosmonauts insisted on what they saw and heard and were put in a type of insane asylum for "retraining," as this was just too much for the government leadership to swallow at the time.

What I find amazing is that people tend to focus more on demonic beings that lurk and compete for spheres of authority even in outer space. That is why other astronauts have reported demonic entities when in outer space and even on the moon, etc.

Most the world focuses on the dark side of beings in outer space but forget that they are the counterfeit. God assigned heavenly hosts to run His creation, so demons and dark entities always try to interfere. When I get the privilege of going to outer space, maybe on a commercial flight version of Space X or other, I will be looking for God's messengers, not the devil's.

And I will also be looking for the Glory of God that exists and manifests differently in outer space than it does on earth, just as time is moving at a different speed the farther you get from earth. And of course in Heaven there is no time at all.

Angels of Government

God has opened many doors into government over the years. I received something from Ruth Heflin (a powerful prophetess) in the area of government. (She has since passed on.) Somehow doors would just open to her to speak with presidents and kings and in the Pentagon and even to prophesy to the Pope. One day God revealed to me that there is a glory that God put over government. And in each glory there are angels. When the revelation hit me, within weeks I was ministering to the vice president of an African nation, prophesying to him, confirming many things only he knew, as he wept and prayed with me in tears.

Then I was in the White House and the Israeli embassy in DC prophesying in and praying into the oval office and press room after decreeing the doors to open, when the government glory angel came around me for about three minutes.

Another time the United Nations opened up. As God told me to decree, it opened when the same angelic glory hovered over me during a prayer time. Inside the UN I was speaking and prophesying about a secret meeting that was occurring simultaneously in another room to try and push a vote to divide Israel, which was stopped at the time but later confirmed.

Another time this door opened again was years ago while in Vanuatu as I prayed with the president for his healing in his office. I also ministered prophetically to the prime minister as he attended the outdoor evangelistic event, and he even shared a few words the last night.

Another time while I was in another Asian nation, I prophesied over the nation and the future issues they would need to contend with. Only a few days later while in Washington, DC, I unexpectedly ran into the vice president of that Asian nation on February 6, 2020, at a Presidential Prayer Breakfast and gave him a word regarding the future of his nation in contention with another powerful nation. He immediately thanked me and said he knew it was important to get this word to the president upon his return.

While in a particular country in Africa, I received seven issues that nation needed to beware of. I began to decree the doors to open. About three *hours* before our flight home, the door opened as I discovered my hotel was located right next to the presidential headquarters. We were able to go directly to the governmental house (their version of the White House) to deliver God's word and prophesy over their nation and what they needed to do. The timing was very urgent as major events and issues would unfold shortly after this word.

I could go on about seeing these government doors open while in many other nations, some of which I cannot share in a book for obvious reasons of security and protecting the leaders. But the main point I want to share is that I believe there were angels of government that opened these doors for me.

Paul was able to go to the world rulers and religious leaders of his day. He was an apostle, which is a heavenly government position. Angels helped pave the way for him to minister to the ruler of Cypress and lead him to salvation after his opposition was defeated when the sorcerer Bar-Jesus went blind (Acts 13:6-12).

Another time Paul ministered to the ruling jailer over the entire prison after an earthquake (Acts 16:23-30). Yet another time, while a prisoner, he acquired an audience with the chief of the island of Malta who received healing. Revival hit the entire island and Paul was actually celebrated, going from prisoner to leader (Acts 28:1-10).

Paul continued his journey, determined to go to Rome to speak before the emperor of the most powerful world empire at the time (Acts 25:10-12). Faith in God's ability to open these doors via angels is also key.

End-Time Deception—Fallen Angels

In the end times there will be great deception. The Bible mentions that if it were possible, even the very elect could be deceived if God did not shorten the days. Matthew 24:24-25 (NLT): *"For false messiahs and false prophets will rise up and perform great signs and wonders so as to deceive, if possible, even God's chosen ones. See, I have warned you about this ahead of time."*

The counterfeit to working with God's angels are the fallen angels and demons of our day. The Bible says that even satan can masquerade as an angel of light. What are some of the end-time deceptions to watch out for? A major end-time deception is the "Alien UFO" phenomena. The world would have you think that there are green or grey aliens living on other planets and visiting earth in space ships that have a higher spirituality than humans and are here to help our planet before we self-destruct. Many Hollywood movies have tried to slowly deceive the masses in believing this. Many think that there are good and bad aliens or beings from outer space. And even parts of the Catholic Church say that if aliens exist we might need to be baptized by them, etc. The entire scenario is a huge deception.

Add to this the UFO or UAP's (Unidentified Flying Objects and Unidentified Anomalous Phenomena) and the supposed cover-up by the government that we are being visited by aliens. This then would lead to the supposition, which parts of the Vatican have eluded to, saying that the passage in Genesis of "Let us make man in our image" is referring to aliens seeding the earth and that we are their offspring.

The truth is that there are no aliens living on other planets. What does exist are fallen angels, watchers from the book of Genesis and demons that can masquerade as aliens to mimic Hollywood movies.

These are actually inter-dimensional demonic spirits. They can enter our dimension and then disappear. That's why many of the supposed UFOs that even military pilots have tried to chase or shoot at say it's like they are not physical and can go 1,000 mph, take a sharp turn, then suddenly disappear.

The fallen angels from before the flood that mixed with human daughters were once worshipped on earth. These same demonic spirits still want to be worshipped. The enemy is trying to set up the world for a great deception that these beings from other dimensions are here to help us and give us great knowledge and technology. What's interesting is it sounds so much like the Garden of Eden when the serpent tempted Eve to gain knowledge by eating the fruit from the Tree of the Knowledge of Good and Evil instead of eating from the Tree of Life.

Many Christians are fascinated by UFOs and sightings of creatures like Big Foot and other odd occurrences. It's not that these things are not happening, but the *source* of these things is the real question.

As I write this, suddenly there are more UFO and strange drone and orb sightings in the skies over the United States than at any other time—even being reported on the nightly news. Newscasters, podcasters, and interviews with Air Force pilots now openly say that the intel they are getting could be from other planets or high-level technology not yet revealed. Most sightings are high-tech drones.[6]

The USA and China are the two main nations that have access to antigravity technology. And 95 percent of all sightings are high-tech drones, military craft, or computer-generated imagery (CGI). Only about 5 percent are actually demonic spirit beings. The dark global governments are trying to mimic that 5 percent demonic using high-tech drones and CGI that can make it look like aliens are coming down or even fake a false return of a Messiah figure. That's how advanced the technology is. Also, artificial intelligence (AI) videos can look so real and yet be so fake at the same time. We need to use major discernment when considering all that we see.

But if you *do* happen to encounter a demonic inter-dimensional being, you are equipped with the highest power and authority in the universe to cast it away, far away!

Sedona UFO Story

While we were still living in Sedona, Arizona, we had some interesting experiences. Sedona is known as a "New Age" center and also known for many sightings of UFOs and orbs. God used us for 12 years ministering to the many lost people there searching for truth and spirituality. We had bought a fixer-upper home on a hill. We hired some men to help us gut the kitchen and put in a new one as well as do some tile work. The men were sleeping at the house during the week before we moved in. One day the manager of the project told me the guys did not want to sleep in the home anymore because they said they saw a spacecraft come right up to the balcony and they were scared.

The next week a carpenter was at the house putting in cabinets, and he too decided not to stay the night. I knew right away it was the demonic realm trying to scare off the workers. When we moved in shortly after, I prayed every night on the balcony overlooking the mountains as the stars were in full array. Every night I worshipped and said out loud, "Okay, show me what you've got!" to whatever was out there scaring off my workers. Never once in three years of living there did anything remotely show up. Why? Because the spirit realm knows born-again believers carry the highest power in the name and blood of Jesus! People who are either overly mesmerized by demonic entities or fear them seem to be the most apt to have these encounters.

I have never heard of a born-again, Spirit-filled believer being abducted and experimented on by these beings, because they know full well these beings have no power over a believer. We need to be aware of these things but not afraid or in awe of them. Many believers and even ministers tend to shy away from this subject, but we should be the authority on all subjects dealing with the supernatural and be able to explain to both the church and the world what these beings are and what they are not.

They are *not* our saviors or messiahs to help the world with new knowledge and technology from another planet. They are fallen angels and demonic entities pretending to be something else so that we will either fear them or give them access to "help" us. Humankind has been given dominion over the earth. The only way satan and his demonic fallen angels have a way into our world is if we invite them in.

At the European Organization for Nuclear Research (CERN) in Switzerland, scientists have been experimenting in opening a wormhole in the fabric of time and space with their hadron collider.

They say that they are seeing entities coming through these portals as they are experimenting. It has been said that some of these scientists are also involved in dark magic and demonic rituals often performed after hours at the same location in CERN.

We are entering a period of the end times when the natural and supernatural world will collide. We will see the operation of God's angels like never before—but we will also see the demonic and fallen angels in operation like never before. We have to discern which are from God and which are deceiving spirits from the enemy's camp.

First Timothy 4:1 (NIV) says, "*The Spirit clearly says that in later times some will abandon the faith and follow deceiving spirits and things taught by demons.*"

Great Deception in the Last Days

Just as there will be a great harvest of souls at the end of the age the likes the world has never seen, there will also be great deception and a great falling away. A time when many will turn from the faith.

> *For false Christs and false prophets will arise, and they will show great signs and wonders so as to deceive and lead astray, if possible, even the elect (God's chosen ones). See, I have warned you beforehand* (Matthew 24:24-25 AMPC).

The Spirit clearly says that in later times some will abandon the faith and follow deceiving spirits and things taught by demons.

So we know some of the deceptions can be tied to the whole UFO deception. Other even more subtle deceptions can be due to not understanding the Scriptures or not being like the sons of Issachar who knew the times and seasons they were in.

We know many in the Western churches are not as on fire as many in the persecuted church or poorer areas of the world. Those enduring persecution know their time to go to Heaven could be at any time; where as in the West, we see most things as very far into the future, including our time to leave this earth. Sometimes this causes a laziness spiritually in seeking the Lord, seeking the Scriptures, living holy, fasting, sharing our faith, etc. Also many end-time events are already happening now that most people were taught they would not see, as they would be raptured out of here before any major end-times events would occur as recorded in the Bible.

Many don't expect to see the Ezekiel 38 war of Gog and Magog, which could very well be sooner than we think, or the third temple being built, for example. Also, most don't expect a worldwide currency or mark of the beast system to occur while they are still here.

They don't expect they would have to be tested in that way. *"And they have defeated him by the blood of the Lamb and by their testimony. And they did not love their lives so much that they were afraid to die"* (Revelation 12:11 NLT). Many assumed that these things would only be required after the rapture for those who missed it—not realizing there are more martyrs today for Christ than at any other time, and we should be ready to be tested even unto death now, not just in the end of the end times.

Many people worldwide are becoming martyrs every day for their faith. I wonder how many believers in the West have truly counted the cost and would not deny their faith if it meant losing their life.

Could a great falling away and deception occur because many today thought these things would never happen or they would not be tested in this way while they are alive on earth? Perhaps the timelines are a bit different from what they understood, and some things *do* happen while they are still here. Will they abandon the faith saying, "I didn't sign up for this! I signed up for salvation, healing, and prosperity only—and then I was supposed to get out of here before life gets too hard."

7

ACCELERATING THE GLORY

There are ways to speed up the Glory of God. But first we need to understand how the Glory of God works.

When someone says, "Wow, the Glory of God is really moving in this place," what are they really saying? When the Glory and Spirit of God is moving, it moves in a circular pattern. The faster it's moving, the more manifestations start to occur. The earthly realm is a mirror of the heavenly realm.

Revelation 7:11 (NIV) tells us, *"All the angels were standing **around** the throne and **around** the elders and the four living creatures. They fell down on their faces before the throne and worshiped God."*

The word *around* means in a circular pattern. Everything that has speed, flight, and acceleration works in circular patterns. We see the earth is moving in a circular pattern around the sun, so are the other planets in our galaxy. Atoms are moving in circular patterns. Cars and planes use engines and propellers that move in circular motion to gain speed and flight.

In fact, could it be that the blueprint for aircraft is found in Ezekiel?

Ezekiel 1:16-21 (NIV) says:

> *This was the appearance and structure of the wheels: They sparkled like topaz, and all four looked alike. Each appeared to be made like a wheel intersecting a wheel. As they moved, they would go in any one of the four directions the creatures faced; the wheels did not change direction as the creatures went. Their rims were high and awesome, and all four rims were full of eyes all around. When the living creatures moved, the wheels beside them moved; and when the living creatures rose from the ground, the wheels also rose. Wherever the spirit would go, they would go, and the wheels would rise along with them, because the spirit of the living creatures was in the wheels. When the creatures moved, they also moved; when the creatures stood still, they also stood still; and when the creatures rose from the ground, the wheels rose along with them, because the spirit of the living creatures was in the wheels.*

Speaking of flight or being transported supernaturally, which I've experienced several times, this also is connected to the Spirit moving in an accelerated circular pattern. When Elijah was taken to Heaven in a whirlwind, that was caused by the Spirit moving in circular patterns creating the heavenly whirlwind. All whirlwinds move in a circular pattern. The faster the movement, like that of a hurricane or tornado, the more things can take flight in the way of the hurricane or tornado moving at a high circular speed.

The devil always likes to copy God and what he knew in Heaven and how things worked and operated. Those involved in the occult, satanism, and New Age often use circles in their group chants, incantations, and prayers.

So how do you get the Spirit to move? It's one thing to create an atmosphere to get the Glory of God to come. Then it's another thing to see the moving of God's Glory! You can have the Glory of God come and descend on a person or a meeting but still not see any manifestation or change. That comes once the Glory of God is moving.

In Genesis, the Spirit or Glory of God was not just present but hovering over the waters. *Hovering* denotes a vibrating sound wave that is moving. The Spirit of God was moving (usually in circular pattern) over the earth and causing a vibrating sound over the waters. Then from here is when you see the manifestation of the creative power of God over the earth. But what causes the Spirit to move? Here is a key.

According to the book of Job, God asked, "*Where were you when I laid the earth's foundation? ...while the morning stars sang together and all the angels shouted for joy?*" (Job 38:4,7 NIV). This passage indicates that the angels were present and worshipping God during the creation of earth.

One key is praise and worship.

Increasing the Speed of Glory

Praise and worship.

Praise and worship is one of the keys to seeing the glory speed up and move at a higher velocity. Why does every church service worldwide always start with praise and worship before the preaching of the Word is released and before the manifestations of God appear? The reason is praise and worship are the foundation for maintaining and the moving of the Glory of God. In

Heaven, which has the highest glory, there is 24/7 praise and worship.

Even King David had 24/7 worship referred to as the Tabernacle of David, as he discovered a pattern from Heaven to keep the glory abiding and moving in Israel during his reign.

When you praise and worship God, you start to sense a change in the atmosphere and even in your own body. Many people report being healed just after praising and worshipping God. We were created to worship Him!

Praise and worship increases the speed of the vibrational frequency of the Glory of God. The faster God is moving, the more powerful things become. Healing and miracles seem to be much more accessible and prevalent after a session of praise and worship.

I remember in Bible school when I got sick with bronchitis during the winter, which I would often get as a teenager. It didn't help being on the ski team in the mountains of northern Arizona, but being ill in Dallas, Texas, seemed so odd. The Lord told me to praise, worship, and dance in my dorm room. I could barely stand up and was sweating profusely because I was sick, so singing and dancing to the Lord seemed impossible. But I obeyed and mustered the little strength I had and started to praise, worship, and dance in my room until I collapsed, passed out on my bed until the next morning.

Amazingly and thankfully, I woke up totally healed! Usually I would be sick for more than a week while taking antibiotics. But that morning, my body resonated with the frequency of Heaven via praise and worship that sped up my miracle.

Your blood carries the memory of both sickness and blessing. If sin or sickness patterns are not put under the blood, you will continue to become ill. But if you focus on the memories of blessings and callings in your bloodline, God can break the cycle and patterns of sickness, failure, fear, sin, and any negative consequences of the Fall of humankind.

Things you tend to do when you are in the flesh are almost pre-programmed and on a default mechanism unless you break the cycle with the blood of Jesus! You can be born again yet still deal with issues in your flesh that have not yet been totally rooted out. The memory in your bloodline in the natural via a blood test can show sickness or even the possibility of sickness in your family history. On another level, family sins are often passed down generationally and can rise up perpetually.

As mentioned earlier, we have seen people set free and healed during Communion services of certain strongholds and patterns. There are always two natures at work. Sin patterns can also be called iniquity. Sin is the action, and iniquity is the pattern of sin. That's why you need to not only to be forgiven of a sin, but you also need to ask God to break the pattern or the iniquity from reoccurring. You can also ask God to break off such things as sickness, poverty, and torment.

Communion

Applying the blood and body of Jesus via Communion is also another powerhouse that speeds up the Glory of God. The blood opens up the portals of Heaven. When you take the blood and body of Jesus, asking Him to cleanse you and repenting of anything in your life not pleasing to Him, it increases the Glory of God and opens the heavenly realm to another level! When God the Father sees the blood and you partake of this, it activates the covenant and promises of God on so many levels. Not only do we see people set free from sinful bondages, healings and miracles and even deliverances can occur while taking Communion.

In Romans 7:24-25 (NIV) Paul writes, "*What a wretched man I am! Who will rescue me from this body that is subject to death? Thanks be to God, who delivers me through Jesus Christ our Lord! So then, I myself in my mind am a slave to God's law, but in my sinful nature a slave to the law of sin.*"

God wants to set us free from all patterns of sin, which is called iniquity. Sin is the act. It is the iniquity found in our bloodline that God wants to totally deliver us from! Why do some believers and even some ministers who love Jesus somehow fall into grave sin? Some of them have not let the blood of Jesus do its full work, as we are to work out our salvation with fear and trembling before the Lord.

Romans 8:11 (NIV) says: "*And if the Spirit of him who raised Jesus from the dead is living in you, he who raised Christ from the dead will also give life to your mortal bodies because of his Spirit who lives in you.*"

Resurrection power can get infused all over your body! The Spirit of holiness and righteousness living in you resets your life. Also, God can break the sin nature in you that is often passed down the family line. Patterns of sin in families can be disrupted by the DNA of the blood of Jesus.

Also, dormant abilities, blessings, and gifts can be awakened that were in your bloodline but left unused or neglected. How often do we see unsaved people even drug addicts suddenly saved, set free, and operating in both natural and spiritual gifts that they did not see before they were saved. The blood of Jesus saved them and awakened dormant gifts, callings and abilities that were in their bloodline all along. I tested this by asking God to not only break any generational patterns or curses in my bloodline, which I have done many times before just to be safe, but I also started to ask Him to open up generational blessings that I had not had activated before but that were in my bloodline.

Suddenly the next morning, during that period between sleeping and waking up, I started to see equations and somehow understood them. And in my half-asleep phase, I whispered to my wife, "I think I understand time travel...." She was a bit surprised. I then realized that my great-grandfather on my Jewish dad's side was a scientist and perhaps his understanding of equations had been passed down to me.

Then I decided to learn hard languages including Russian and others. I picked up the languages super-fast, and people told me I had an almost perfect accent too. Another relative, my great-grandfather whom I had not met, spoke 12 languages and had read newspapers in all those languages before and during World War II in Europe. I was somehow tapping into some of the dormant abilities that were in my bloodline but had been left inactivated. I used Communion with the blood and body of Jesus and asked God to not only break off any generational curses but also to liberate generational blessings from the memory in my blood with the blood of Jesus activating it!

If there is memory in our blood, how much more the memory of the blood of Jesus! The same power and memory of the blood of Jesus hitting our blood can cause resurrection power to course through our being!

I've heard stories of people who had a heart transplant, and after the operation they could fluently speak another language they had never learned. Some believe the memory in the blood of the new heart they received, carried with it memory from the other person via the blood.

I also heard a story of a scientist who had a dog that died and he cloned his dog that he loved. The cloned dog seemed to know the same tricks that the original dog knew and even the routes the scientist would take him when walking in the woods.

If this is true, it would also make sense given the revelation about memory in the blood.

I believe that the mutation in our bloodline called sin can be offset and deactivated and even deleted from the hard drive of the DNA in our blood—and restored by the blood of Jesus and the memory in His blood.

Fasting

Fasting is one of the most underutilized superchargers in increasing the Glory of God. It sensitizes your spirit to see and hear what God is saying and doing. It's so much easier to access the supernatural when fasting. The apostles fasted when they needed to choose a new apostle.

Often I have fasted before a major international crusade or outreach and consequently I saw amazing results! The first time I did a longer fast was while a missionary in France; I fasted 21 days. A short time later I was preaching a six-month revival in a church in the Paris region, it was one of the longest-running revivals in decades in France. The Lord showed me that my fasting is what prepared the ground both for me and the revival itself to ignite. On top of this, I asked the church that invited me to do a 40-day fasting chain. Initially I was invited to speak for four nights, and yet it went for six months straight! In each service new souls were saved and healings, miracles, and deliverances occurred!

Fasting also is necessary when dealing with higher-level demonic strongholds or when seeing God advance in new territories.

The book of Daniel explains how Daniel fasted 21 days, which led to the angelic visitation that told him his prayers were being answered to see Israel set free from bondage. The angel explained that because of his prayers, the angel was able to break through and deal with the prince of Persia who was trying to block him.

This means that our prayers and fasting gives fuel and ammunition and greater power to angels to break through on our behalf. This is because God gives humans authority over the earth. When we intercede and fast and pray, in essence we are giving angels the invitation to work on our behalf for God's Kingdom.

Also when we are fasting, it's a form of humbling ourselves before the Lord in prayer. In fact, the entire nation of Nineveh was saved after they fasted and prayed with repentance when the prophet warned them of imminent destruction due to their sins. From the king to even the animals, the entire nation fasted and repented—and the judgment at that time was called off.

The first mention of the Glory of God was in the Garden of Eden before Adam and Eve sinned. The first sin that caused them to lose the glory covering around them was over food. They ate fruit that they were not supposed to eat, causing them to lose the glory. So in a sense when you fast from food, you are going back to the Garden and reversing and reopening a portal of glory.

Daniel convinced the king's guard to let him and his friends fast; they would not eat the king's meat for a season to prove that it would not diminish their health or abilities in any way. So Daniel and his friends started with a 10-day fast. His fast was a bit different as instead of no food, he ate only vegetables, which now is known as a Daniel Fast.

After this first fast, the men were healthy. In fact, Daniel 1:15 (NIV) tells us, *"At the end of the ten days they looked healthier and better nourished than any of the young men who ate the royal food.*" After the guard saw they looked even better than before, he permitted them to continue with a longer fast.

Daniel 1:16-17 (NIV) says, "*So the guard took away their choice food and the wine they were to drink and gave them vegetables instead. To these four young men God gave knowledge and understanding of all kinds of literature and learning. And Daniel could understand visions and dreams of all kinds.*"

Imagine that, after the fast it was noted that their countenance and even their mental abilities and IQ were much higher than the other men in the king's service. In fact, they were ten times smarter in all areas:

> *The king talked with them, and he found none equal to Daniel, Hananiah, Mishael and Azariah; so they entered the king's service. In every matter of wisdom and understanding about which the king questioned them, he found them* ***ten times better*** *than all the magicians and enchanters in his whole kingdom* (Daniel 1:19-20 NIV).

God gave them knowledge and understanding of all literature and learning! This means not just in the Bible but learning in all areas, which would include math, science, history, and government. And spiritually they also excelled, as Daniel could understand visions and dreams of all kinds!

I believe fasting opens realms of Glory that can cause our physical body, our mental abilities, and our spiritual senses to be upgraded to a major level! God can increase your IQ during fasting! It is said that we use less than 10 percent of our brain capacity. Could it be since the Fall of Adam and Eve something in our brain was shut down and our physical bodies and spiritual abilities affected, causing humans to die much younger than was originally intended? And could it be equally possible that fasting can tap into both spiritual, mental, and physical dormant abilities that could not be reached without it?

Giving

Giving should be a normal part of the Christian life. When we are continual givers it can open not just natural but supernatural blessings. In fact, it's recorded that when Cornelius gave to help God's people, he was visited by an angel as a portal in Heaven opened and he heard these words recorded in Acts 10:4 (NIV), *"Cornelius stared at him in fear. 'What is it, Lord?' he asked. The angel answered, 'Your prayers and gifts to the poor have come up as a memorial offering before God.'"*

When you combine these different keys to accelerate the glory, a fusion of accelerated glory starts to manifest. It's like having your car run on all eight cylinders instead of just one or two. Some people focus more on prayer and fasting, for others it's mostly praise and worship, others walk in the blood and holiness daily, while others are amazing givers. You can excel in any one of these areas without activating the other areas—which keeps you from reaching the full quantum levels of glory by combining the different elements. God wants us to walk in it all! Each of us has a different aspect and degree of Glory, but when you combine as many as possible, you receive more of the fullness of the Glory of God.

In Cornelius' case, he combined constant prayer with sacrificial giving to the people of God. And even more amazing, this led him to become the first Gentile convert to believe in Jesus!

King Solomon gave 1,000 animals as a sacrifice to God, which caused the Lord to visit him and ask him what he wanted. How would you like to have the Lord ask you what you want, instead of you always asking the Lord for something? Solomon's giving in such an extravagant way drew God's attention! Solomon asked for wisdom, which led to the Lord giving Solomon his desire and he became the most wise of any man on planet Earth. And because Solomon asked for wisdom—not riches, military power, fame, or selfish desires—God gave him all those things as well, making him the richest king ever. His giving led to an open-heaven portal.

Even the widow who gave her last two very small copper coins is mentioned in our Bibles (Mark 12:41-44 NIV); because it was all she had, this was a sacrificial offering. The widow giving Elijah her last meal also was a sacrifice, but she did it. This led to her and her son not dying of famine and also receiving a word to get as many vessels as possible so God could multiply the costly oil. Her obedience lifted her out of poverty and even led to the resurrection of her son later on.

The woman who washed Jesus' feet with her hair after breaking an alabaster box of perfume worth a year's wages, spent it all on Jesus. This act of love was symbolic of God anointing Jesus to prepare Him for His soon-coming crucifixion and resurrection. Of course the woman, Mary, became born again and followed Jesus. It also led later to her brother Lazarus being raised from the dead.

John 11:1-2,40,43-44 (NIV) tells us:

> *Now a man named Lazarus was sick. He was from Bethany, the village of Mary and her sister Martha.*

(This Mary, whose brother Lazarus now lay sick, was the same one who poured perfume on the Lord and wiped his feet with her hair.) …Then Jesus said, "Did I not tell you that if you believe, you will see the glory of God?" …When he had said this, Jesus called in a loud voice, "Lazarus, come out!" And the dead man came out….

8

GLORY'S SOUND AND LIGHT

In the beginning God created the heavens and the earth. Now the earth was formless and empty, darkness was over the surface of the deep, and the Spirit of God was hovering over the waters. And God said, "Let there be light," and there was light

(Genesis 1:1-3 NIV).

I believe thoughts at a certain level can also be a form of communication in the spirit realm.

Many have testified, having died and returned to life, that in Heaven much communication is done via thoughts. And in Heaven all is laid bare and clear.

The Bible says God can do abundantly more than what we ask or think. Most people ask God but don't see it in their thoughts and minds, but the Bible says to both ask and think. Think on these things that the Bible mentions. So thinking is not a sin, actually God encourages us to think His thoughts that are noble, righteous, just, and of good report.

We need to tune in to fully access all the Jesus died and paid for. Because of the Fall, humans only use a very small percentage of our brains, so imagine what Adam and Eve were able to think and do before the fall.

According to Scharl van Staden: "When the sound that resonates out of the heart of God's people comes into agreement with the sound resonating after God's heart, we find worship on earth as it is in heaven. There was a reason Jesus only did and said what He saw His Father doing....it wasn't just about obedience but about resonance and the power of being aligned frequentially and vibrationally."[7] And I add ...with the rhythm of Heaven.

Jesus only did what He saw and heard. So we too need to start to see in the spirit what Heaven is doing and authorizing, and then just do that. That's why Jesus was so successful—because He only did what He saw and heard from God. Most people just do things for God, and it's often hit and miss, not being led by the Holy Spirit. Or maybe someone takes a class on how to heal the sick or how to cast out demons or interpret dreams, but the person can still go through the motions and not have the same results as when they tune in to the frequency of Heaven and what Jesus is doing and saying at that particular moment.

Often in my meetings God will ask me to release a word of healing or a word of knowledge that seems so out there but if I just obey it, it occurs. One lady in France, who was very well dressed with a major back issue and possibly needed surgery, came up after I gave the word of knowledge. Then the Lord told me to throw a glass of very cold water in her face. I really hesitated, but as I obeyed and she felt the cold water, she was immediately and supernaturally thrown to the ground. When she got up, she was totally healed. Her doctor confirmed this and was amazed at the miracle.

Other times it's a word to give to a president or a prime minister to decree the door to open. It's one thing to have faith for the door to open and led by the Holy Spirit to declare it, and it's another thing to be in the presence of leaders of nations and releasing a word that only they know if it's from God.

This occurred while in Vanuatu when I prayed with the president for healing and ministered prophetically to the prime minister there. Another time while I was in Taiwan I prophesied over the nation and the future issues they would need to contend with. Only a few days later in Washington, DC, I unexpectedly ran into the vice president of Taiwan on February 6, 2020, at a Presidential Prayer Breakfast and give him a word regarding the future of Taiwan in relation to China and depending on Taiwan's continued closeness with Israel, etc. He immediately wrote this down and said he knew it was important to get this word to the president upon his return.

Recently while in Kenya, I received seven issues Kenya needed to beware of. I began to decree the doors open. About three hours before our flight home, the door opened and I discovered my hotel was right next to the presidential headquarters. We were able to go directly to the first lady to deliver the word and prophesy over their nation and what they needed to do. The timing was very urgent as major events and issues would unfold shortly after this word.

The key is hearing the sound of Heaven and doing what we see the Father doing as Jesus did. Then things really flow. Practicing hearing and staying at the highest frequency of Heaven's glory as possible is key. I listed some of these steps in the previous chapter, such as fasting, praise and worship, and the blood. Once in the high glory, you decree the sound of the word you are hearing in the glory, and that higher frequency of the sound of glory will suddenly start to break open the barriers and pierce the thin veil between Heaven and earth. Basically, the glory plus sound equals created manifestations.

You take those things from the invisible realm that you can see in the spirit while in the glory, and decree what you see God doing—then He takes those invisible particles and brings them into this physical reality.

Let me say it this way, faith is the substance, or subatomic atom or particle, of things hoped for. So when you decree with the sound of Heaven's glory what the Father is saying, He will take the sound you are speaking and from the invisible realm form the visible. The invisible realm is what creates the visible realm. Just like in Genesis, God used two invisible substances to create solid matter.

The first ingredient was the Spirit of the Glory of God. You cannot see it, but it's real. The second ingredient was sound. Though sound is invisible, when it is mixed with the glory it produces physical substance. And if you believe what God is decreeing through you, it starts to manifest on the subatomic level right away! The moment you command cancer to die while hearing God tell you to say it while in the heavy glory, the cancer is affected. Sometimes you see immediate results, and sometimes you have to keep speaking to the cancer to whittle it down until it no longer can survive and eventually dies.

It's not so much someone speaking words to sickness alone, but it's from what dimension of glory and Heaven they are speaking from. You can tell the difference in levels of authority coming from levels of intimacy with Jesus from person to person. Words or sound alone is not enough. It must be coming from a place of having been in the presence of His Glory.

We all have a sound emanating out of us that is as unique as a fingerprint or a snowflake. We were created to worship Him.

Also the entire creation was created to worship Him and everything created has a sound that worships God. Inside the atom of everything created there is a vibrating sound wave called a quark. This quark releases a sound that is a praise to God. The Bible confirms this truth that every living thing has a sound—and it is worship.

Let's look at Psalm 148 (NIV):

> *Praise the Lord. Praise the Lord from the heavens; praise him in the heights above. Praise him, all his angels; praise him, all his heavenly hosts. Praise him, sun and moon; praise him, all you shining stars. Praise him, you highest heavens and you waters above the skies. Let them praise the name of the Lord, for at his command they were created, and he established them for ever and ever—he issued a decree that will never pass away. Praise the Lord from the earth, you great sea creatures and all ocean depths, lightning and hail, snow and clouds, stormy winds that do his bidding, you mountains and all hills, fruit trees and all cedars, wild animals and all cattle, small creatures and flying birds, kings of the earth and all nations, you princes and all rulers on earth, young men and women, old men and children. Let them praise the name of the Lord, for his name alone is exalted; his splendor is above the earth and the heavens. And he has raised up for his people a horn, the praise of all his faithful servants, of Israel, the people close to his heart. Praise the Lord.*

That's why often you can feel the presence of God when you are in raw nature, hiking in the mountains, watching huge waterfalls, enjoying the first snow, and even while hearing thunder and lightning; there is a glory that electrifies your being. The reason is because your spirit can pick up the sound of praise coming off of creation! Let everything that has breath praise the Lord!

9

THINKING IN THE GLORY FOR BREAKTHROUGH

Is it really possible to say and think what you desire and it manifests? According to Scripture it is. Proverbs 23:7 (NKJV) says, *"For as he thinks in his heart, so is he."* Mark 11:23 (NKJV) says, *"For assuredly, I say to you, whoever says to this mountain, 'Be removed and be cast into the sea,' and does not doubt in his heart, but believes that those things he says will be done, he will have whatever he says."*

Those in unsaved circles who are trying to be spiritual often refer to this principle as the law of attraction. The idea behind this "law" is everything that you desire is attracted to you by images in your mind and thoughts and spoken words. It is one of the most talked about philosophies in the world in both motivational teaching as well as other spiritual groups.

Oddly enough, it only works on a limited scale for most people, if at all, because of the origins and the foundation from which these laws are derived. It is actually a deeper spiritual law that is derived from these two Scriptures and others, but when taken out of context, it does not produce the ultimate desired results. "Pseudo spiritual" groups took this principle from Scriptures such as Mark 11:23 and Proverbs 23:7 and excluded God as the ultimate Source of the provision. It makes the person God instead of humbling the person and connecting to the Creator, the Giver of all things.

In 2 Samuel chapter 11, the Bible tells the story of King David, a man after God's heart (Acts 13:22), who saw a woman named Bathsheba bathing on her roof. She was lovely to behold, and he was immediately drawn to her. Even though she was married, he started a relationship with her, she became pregnant, and David had her husband killed in an attempt to cover his tracks. He got what he looked at, but he did not anticipate the outcome.

God was not pleased, and their son died. David used this similar principle of thinking and seeing a desire and then obtaining it, but on a much lower level, which produced results with major consequences because it was governed by wrong motives and for his own selfish purposes. So using this principle not connected to the Creator and only thinking and imagining what we think we want will not yield desirable results.

Imagine your friend gets a new car, and you decide you want one too, so you implement the "law of attraction" by thinking about it, visiting the car lot, and displaying pictures of the car all around you. Finally, you get the car, but it comes with a price because you now have a car loan you cannot afford. You used the principle for selfish gain, and like David, it did not end well for you.

You can really manifest the life you are called to live by using the authority He gave us of speaking and thinking His words and thoughts—but you must be mindful to do it God's way. Jesus said that He only did what He saw the Father do (John 5:19). That means the key to using this principle is to first hear God, and then use the spiritual law to help bring about whatever He tells you to do.

Thoughts Create

We know from science that speaking can have a positive or negative effect on objects and creative matter. Thoughts can as well. Whether negatively or positively, thoughts impact your world physiologically, emotionally, and spiritually. You should decide now how your thoughts will affect your life and the lives of those around you. Philippians 4:8 (NKJV) says, "*Finally, brethren, whatever things are true, whatever things are noble, whatever things are just, whatever things are pure, whatever things are lovely, whatever things are of good report, if there is any virtue and if there is anything praiseworthy—meditate on these things.*" Why did Paul say this? Because he understood that thoughts create!

Have you ever watched an intense, action-filled movie as someone drives off a cliff? Your body sends signals to your mind as if it is actually happening to you. You start to perspire, and your heart starts racing because your eyes are watching, but your body cannot differentiate if what you are seeing is real or not. Consistent meditation on something such as a painful childhood memory can also cause negative physiological changes in your body. When unpleasant thoughts germinate in your mind, toxins are released into your bloodstream, weakening your immune system and affecting your blood sugar levels.

If watching a movie, dreaming, or thinking can cause adverse physiological changes, imagine what would happen if you used your mind to think on things that are lovely and of good report by intentionally thinking and seeing by faith in your mind and spirit what you are praying for. God gave us an imagination to use for good, not for evil or to waste. You do not have to wait until you have a dream at night. You can on purpose close your eyes and envision yourself with your prayers answered and see them come to pass.

Ephesians 3:20 (NKJV) says, "*Now to Him who is able to do exceedingly abundantly above all that we ask* ***or think,*** *according to the power that works in us.*" As I meditated on this Scripture, it occurred to me that thinking as well as asking will manifest what I'm believing for according to His will.

One time I felt a strong desire from God to go to Australia. I did not pray about it or even tell anyone I wanted to go, but for weeks and weeks I could not shake the thought that I was supposed to go to Australia. At the time, I was preparing to go to Vanuatu, an island in the South Pacific. The only way to get there is to go through Australia.

For three days, the desire to go to Australia weighed heavier and heavier on me each day. On the third day, I received an email from someone in Australia asking me to please come and speak at two national events that November. That was the exact month I was going to Vanuatu. It worked out perfectly. My wife and I flew through Sydney and presented the gospel at several major national events in Melbourne and Perth in Australia while on the way to Vanuatu.

I encourage you to learn to incorporate thoughts into your prayers. If you pray for an hour, spend another hour with soft, soaking music, seeing yourself with whatever you just prayed for. It is not wrong to imagine yourself with what God said you could have. There is no such thing as an idle brain, you are always thinking whether you realize it or not. So why not intentionally use your thoughts to see your bills paid, your family saved, or your thriving career, business, or ministry.

Picture what you want in your mind according with what you understand His will in your life to be, and the thought will send a signal to what you are thinking about, causing it to manifest.

God wants to do amazing things in and through you. Ask Him what they are and make a commitment to fill your heart and mind with them. Place pictures in your car of whatever you are praying about. Place a picture on your bathroom mirror, your electronic devices, and anywhere you can see it often. Create a framework for your thoughts to manifest and to be in perfect alignment with Heaven.

Expectancy Creates

In my miracle services, I tell people to start looking for the miracle we are praying for immediately. I say over and over, check again, check again, check again because I understand that when you think and/or look for it at a high enough intensity and faith level, it sends a radio signal to the brain causing what you are thinking about to manifest. Have you ever thought about calling a person for a few days and then they call you or you run into them? This is an example of your thoughts and expectancy creating.

Once I was in Topeka, Kansas, speaking to about 700 people, and the presence of God was heavy in the place. Leading up to the meeting, God told me what miracles He will do. In some meetings, we have seen tumors disappear, missing teeth form, and teeth that were grayish black turn to solid bright gold that could have only come from Heaven.

As I spoke, I started decreeing the miracles that I saw in my mind. Suddenly, in my spirit, I saw someone's white hair turning black. I did not have a clue how that would happen or whose hair it was, but I knew the presence and Glory of God combined with speaking into existence what I am seeing created, so I told the crowd what I saw and told everyone to check their hair.

A few minutes later, we heard a woman from the crowd screaming that her husband's hair used to be completely white, but the front had turned black. I asked the man to come up on stage. The hair on the back of his head was still white, but the front was indeed black. It was amazing, but the miracle was not complete. So, without praying, we kept staring at his hair, imagining it was all black. I was not anxious or fearful that the miracle would not happen because there is a passage that says, *"He who has begun a good work in you will complete it"* (Philippians 1:6 NKJV). I just stared at his head like everyone else. Within a few minutes, the rest of his hair started turning black, right in front of me and 700 other people.

When you look for something, you are expecting it to appear. When you are looking at an object, your eyeballs act as a mirror. The object you are looking at can see itself in your eyes, therefore manifesting itself. I told the people to see, by faith, the man with a full head of black hair; so in their minds, they were thinking black hair according to the word of knowledge. The white hair was looking into their eyes, it saw the black hair the people were thinking about and mirrored it, just like unspeckled lambs stared at speckled lambs and reproduced speckled lambs in Genesis 30:31-43. They became what they looked at.

Many other miracles in our meetings happened as people looked for them, including blind eyes opened, deaf ears healed, and a paralytic getting up to see if he could stand—and he started walking.

At a meeting in Jerusalem, miracles were happening all over the place. I sensed that God wanted to do some creative dental work, so I told everyone to check their teeth. A cameraman saw a guy looking in a lady's mouth, so he focused his camera on her mouth. Then I heard gasps emanating from the congregation. I looked up, and on the two big screens behind us, we could see what started as a speck of gold, then a whole gold tooth formed in her mouth. Also, a lady who could not sing before the meeting started belting out notes like Whitney Houston. It was astonishing. Not only did people get saved in that meeting, but several people came up to repent of unbelief and critical spirits.

We have seen God heal many people this way, including those who were crippled, blind, and deaf, people who could not speak, and many other types of expected miracles and even unusual miracles. Even the apostle Paul experienced unusual miracles in addition to the "evangelically accepted" miracles.

We can tell a religious spirit when God does a new miracle and we start to doubt it's from God. This may be because we have not yet encountered such things. I know this because I was one who fought God on some of the newer types of miracles until I died to my religious spirit and fear of what people would say and let God do His works, whether I fully understood them all or not. I knew, though, it was from God by the good fruit it was producing. Very hardened people came to the Lord who did not respond to the Lord before.

Everything is made of atoms. Inside the atoms are protons and neutrons. Inside that is a sound wave. It is a quark, a vibrating sound wave that God put there at creation. Here is how the Creator did it. He thought it then He spoke it, "Let there be light! Let there be sand. Let there be trees," and so on. I believe that at the core of the *let there be* words there is a sound wave. These are vibrating sound waves that create solid matter. When you look to see "if that tooth is turning gold from black," that sound wave can pick up that you are looking at it. As you look at it, it starts to pop, it starts turning gold at the core of the tooth. Eventually showing on the surface what started on the inside.

Take for example and consider that when Elijah spoke that the clouds would produce rain, something started but was not yet seen; then as he sent his servant to keep looking for what he just prophesied would occur, after the seventh time he saw a cloud the size of a man's hand. Soon enough it was pouring rain as the prophet had prophesied.

It's one thing to speak to a body part but then when we start to look for the miracle in faith, it speeds things up. Consider also Ezekiel chapter 37 when he spoke to the bones and they began to move and come together. Speaking is phase one—Ezekiel said as he looked at them, skin covered the bones. *Ask* and it shall be given and *seek* (look) and it shall be found. So many times when people start to test their bodies and actually look for their miracle rather than just get a word for their miracle, the miracles can speed up dramatically.

When you believe for something, diligently search for it until it manifests. Look with an attitude. Have you ever thought about an unsaved loved one you were believing to get saved, or a home or car you were believing God for and then suddenly you start seeing the car or home everywhere? In the original language of the passage, "*...Ask and it shall be given, seek and you will find, knock and the door shall be opened to you,*" it does not mean to just seek once, look once, and ask once then hope for the best. It actually means to seek and keep seeking, to knock and keep knocking, and to look and keep looking until what you are believing for manifests. Expectancy and persistence is key in manifesting the life you desire.

Emotions Create

You can decree, confess, name it, claim it, and pray all the right words, but if you are not emotionally connected to your dreams or desires, you do not really believe they are going to happen. Successful leaders like the founders of Tesla, Apple, and Microsoft were emotionally connected and passionate to the point of obsession with their ideas. Even though he did not get to build it, King David was obsessed with building a temple for the God of Israel. You too should be emotionally connected and righteously obsessed with the vision that God gave you.

Sometimes people hold back from getting too excited about their dreams in fear of being disappointed, but you have to put your emotions, mind, body, and spirit into your God-given dreams and be excited about what you are praying, believing, and speaking until it manifests.

I have heard many stories of clowns and comedians visiting terminally ill cancer patients who, after the jovial visit, experience remission caused from laughter. Can you see how this works? There are a lot of cranky believers and people in general who hold grudges and then wonder why they aren't happy and healthy.

My friend, Sid Roth, is one of the greatest Jewish evangelists, leading many to the Messiah. He is absolutely obsessed with his mission. One time, he and I went to lunch in Charlotte, North Carolina, and he immediately started sharing the gospel with the server, the cook, and everyone he encountered. Before the server took our order, he immediately said, "Are you a believer? Do you know the Messiah?"

"Oh yes. I am from Africa, I am Nigerian," she replied.

"Yes, but are you born again and Spirit-filled, speaking in your heavenly language?" Sid asked.

"Well, I do not have that gift yet."

Sid looked at me and said, "She does not have that gift yet, let's take care of that. This is not a gift for everybody. It is a gift for everybody who is a believer."

Well, we should have ordered first, because after we prayed with her, the power of God slammed her to the floor. Boom! A manager and another lady came out to make sure the server was okay.

"Did she pass out? Is she having a seizure? Does she need medical help?" they asked.

"Oh no," we said. "She's fine. We prayed for her to receive the Holy Spirit. Are you a Spirit-filled believer?"

We didn't eat for more than an hour, which is a normal occurrence when we are together. Sid and I put our heart, soul, and mind into the vision, and our passion creates more and more souls for the Kingdom, connecting people with God, the Giver of life, love, power, health, and peace.

10

END-TIME HARVEST

I recently had an end-time vision of the last-days harvest of souls. I saw this vision during an outdoor crusade in Buenos Aires, Argentina, about one hour from the center of the city. In this vision, I suddenly saw the earth bending almost as if in pain as wars hit one area of the earth. Then in another area, major natural disasters occurred. While yet in another region great economic upheaval was happening, and in another place on earth there was great oppression and persecution.

As I saw massive areas of earth almost groaning in pain, suddenly in other parts, a great, unexpected harvest of souls would start to manifest—some in the most unexpected places and nations where one would not think could have such a harvest of souls. It was like a bumper crop, an historic level of souls being saved. It was almost as if the bending of the earth due to these events was causing a side effect of multiplying and ripening the harvest on earth.

When I came out of the vision, the Lord begin to show me that as the world continues to shake and bend with wars and rumors of wars, natural disasters of earthquakes, hurricanes, floods and fires, famines as well as economic and political upheaval, God was also accelerating the great harvest of souls simultaneously. In fact, I believe that the more we see wars and natural disasters, the more so the gospel will open up to being preached even in the most unreached places on earth.

Matthew 24:6-8 (NIV) tells us, "*You will hear of wars and rumors of wars, but see to it that you are not alarmed. Such things must happen, but the end is still to come. Nation will rise against nation, and kingdom against kingdom. There will be famines and earthquakes in various places. All these are the beginning of birth pains.*"

So I believe I was seeing the earth literally reeling in pain and bending as if someone hit it in the gut. These are the beginnings of birth pains. Birth of what? The birth of the beginning of the end when Jesus will return.

In fact, the disciples asked Jesus the very same question people are asking today. What are the signs of the end times and what are we to look out for, thus the reason for writing this book. Many of these signs are accelerating as never before in our lifetimes as we can see in the next Scripture verses:

> *Then you will be handed over to be persecuted and put to death, and you will be hated by all nations because of me. At that time many will turn away from the faith and will betray and hate each other, and many false prophets will appear and deceive many people. Because of the increase of wickedness, the love of most will grow cold, but the one who stands firm to the end will be saved. And this gospel of the kingdom will be preached in the whole world as a testimony to all nations, and then the end will come* (Matthew 24:9-14 NIV).

The end-time signs and wars is all the talk nowadays, some even predicting World War III. Christian persecution is increasing worldwide and a form of it went to a new level in 2020 during the pandemic when even churches in the USA were forbidden to open, and in some states only 50 people were permitted to gather to worship, sitting six feet apart. In some places people were forbidden to sing and worship together, and some pastors were even persecuted and actually sentenced to jail and threatened by their local governments for daring to open their church doors. Yet bars, large department stores, and strip clubs were permitted to be open and carry on business as usual. During the end times, betrayals will increase and there will be a massive, sudden rise of false prophecies alongside true prophecies, thanks to social media.

Discernment is so needed in these times. The Bible mentions a time of many turning from the faith and betraying other believers when the persecution starts. During the 2020 pandemic some church leaders and congregants reported to the police other nearby churches that chose to meet and pray for those in need. These type of betrayals were foretelling of things to come. But my favorite part of this whole passage is Matthew 24:14 (NIV), *"And this gospel of the kingdom will be preached in the whole world as a testimony to all nations, and then the end will come!"*

I believe the pressures and hardships of these end times will actually cause believers to have to press in that much more into the Lord and stay in His Glory and presence, which will lead to many being drawn and saved as the darkness gets darker—but the light gets brighter in all of us!

Romans 8:18 (NIV) says, *"I consider that our present sufferings are not worth comparing with the glory that will be revealed in us."*

We are to use any and all hardships or sufferings as a springboard to draw us even closer to the Lord, causing the Glory of

God around us to increase more and more, thus drawing more and more people to Jesus!

That is what we are starting to see now! For the past two years, the Lord has been increasing our focus, having us laser focused on the end-time harvest. Even though we have been doing this for the past 34 years, in the last 24 months we have seen more souls saved than at any other time! In fact, as mentioned previously, I preached to more than 1 million unsaved Muslims in two nights in two different cities with more than 500,000 in each city—and 80 to 90 percent of them received salvation! Eyes were opened, many heard and spoke for the first time, paralytics walked, and demon-possessed, screaming people had to be held down. Each later testified of their miracle deliverance. And that was just one of the many nations where we held large evangelistic meetings in 2023.

That same year, we also had many meetings in Israel, with the most souls saved in one service than we had ever seen. There were three gatherings in Argentina, numerous ones in Europe, the Philippines, and many other nations.

This year we will be having open-air, harvest soul-winning events again in Argentina, Colombia, Uruguay, Philippines, Australia, Samoa, Tonga, Israel, and Pakistan. There will be revival meetings in the UK, as well as revival meetings winning the lost in some of the most unreached nations, including Japan and France, all in addition to the numerous meetings across the USA and the meetings we host five times a year at our center in Arizona.

God is speeding up the harvest of souls worldwide as He is in a hurry!

Basically there is a race between God and satan; God wants as many souls as He can reach and save with our cooperation and obedience. At the same time, satan is trying to see how many people he can kill on planet Earth using war, pestilence, famine, and persecution.

Vision of Cities on Fire

I had another vision while speaking at a revival meeting in Southern California. In the vision I was above the United States and I saw fires in different cities spaced out across the nation. I asked the Lord what that meant. He told me these were places and churches, towns and cities where the fire of God was growing into embers of revival.

As I looked, the fires got larger and larger and then the fires started to connect with the other fires. The Lord showed me the apostolic center of revival, prayer, intercession, fasting, evangelism and the power of God being released in healings, miracles, and deliverance. And the more I looked, the bigger these fires became as they connected like dots all across the land to the other fire zones.

The Lord began to show me that the true remnant of God's church on earth will start to connect with each other and work with each other. Not only that, I saw God was even creating supernatural highways between these places full of the Glory of God on fire. So much so that they will invite speakers from each other's revivals to fan the flames. And then I saw that people will even be transported like Philip in between these places of fire. The open heavens in these places created a grid in which these supernatural transportations will take place.

In the enemy's camp, he is creating Freemason powerlines over cities and grids to form a network of many cities on earth, connecting them as "sister cities," along with physical, secret underground passages between these locations. We know the enemy is a copycat and tries to mimic what he knows to be true in the heavenly realm.

Glory Evangelism

In this end-time harvest, the glory will be so key. In fact, the glory will invade entire areas just like when John G. Lake ministered in Spokane, Washington, which made it to be considered the healthiest city in America as so many were healed.

When Charles Finney was approaching a town by train, people at times could feel the glory coming miles away and fall down to repent and give their lives to Jesus. That's the Glory of God! In Pakistan, the glory realm was such that masses of Muslims easily gave their lives to Jesus—and this was even before the miracles—just at the preaching of the Cross, and the death, burial, and resurrection of Jesus as the only way to salvation with the Glory of God present! In Israel, considered one of the hardest places to see souls saved, we have been seeing between 400 to 600 people saved in a single service. Of course God gives us a strategy for each city and place, and when we follow it there is a great harvest!

Many times when I am at a store or gym, people come up to me asking what I have or why I seem to carry something invisible. Often this occurs when I had just finished a fast or just after leaving a revival meeting or after having had an intense time with the Lord in prayer. People can sense and are drawn by the Glory of God, asking me who I am and what I carry. That is glory evangelism.

I, of course, love to do power evangelism where I use the gifts of healing or word of knowledge to get an unsaved person to open up to salvation. But it's a whole new level when the glory saturates me and an area and people are drawn by the glory and basically ask what they must do to be saved. They want what I have, what you have. Then it's even easier to share the gospel, pray for the sick, and lead people to salvation.

I remember just coming off a three-day fast in Sedona, Arizona, and I went to the health food store to break my fast with a healthy soup. I sat in the deli area eating my yummy soup. I could feel the glory and presence of God so strongly. The Lord told me to just inhale and exhale the Glory of God I was sensing.

Little did I know that at the next table was a psychic trying to give a reading to the man in front of her. Suddenly she stopped and turned toward my direction and said to me out loud, "Who are you? Wow, you have a huge aura around you." Often those in the New Age or occult use terms like *aura* as they don't know how to describe what they are seeing, especially when they encounter the Glory of God. The glory can travel beyond yourself and touch people near you.

Look at the story of Peter the apostle. Not only did he pray for and see the sick healed, but at times the Glory of God on him was healing people just by his shadow as he walked down the street.

Acts 5:15-16 (NIV) reveals:

> *As a result, people brought the sick into the streets and laid them on beds and mats so that at least Peter's shadow might fall on some of them as he passed by. Crowds gathered also from the towns around Jerusalem, bringing their sick and those tormented by impure spirits, and all of them were healed.*

Supernatural Transportation

One aspect that is connected to the end-time glory and end-time harvest is supernatural transportation. That is when God suddenly transports you to another location, usually for the gospel. That's why it's connected with the end-time harvest.

> *When they came up out of the water, the Spirit of the Lord suddenly took Philip away, and the eunuch did not see him again, but went on his way rejoicing. Philip, however, appeared at Azotus and traveled about, preaching the gospel in all the towns until he reached Caesarea* (Acts 8:39-40 NIV).

So in this passage Philip is sharing the gospel to an Ethiopian eunuch, most likely Jewish. Many in Ethiopia converted to the God of Israel under the Queen of Sheba who visited King Solomon many years before in the Old Testament. The eunuch was visiting Israel during the feast. Philip shared the gospel with him about the Jewish Messiah and led him to salvation and baptized him. Then suddenly Philip was transported to another city where God wanted him to continue preaching the gospel!

Every time I have been supernaturally transported, it was on the way to preach the gospel and see people saved, healed, and delivered. One time it was in Paris, France, on my way to preach in Belgium about three hours away. My car died because I had put in regular gas instead of the diesel gas that it required. A tow truck finally came and emptied the wrong gas and put in the right gas, but the man warned me that the car still wouldn't work.

I assured him Jesus would heal the car—he laughed, as he was an atheist. As he put in the diesel gas it worked! He was stunned. Then I called the pastor to tell him I would miss the meetings due to car trouble. It was now 7 p.m. and I would arrive around 10 p.m., so I told him to preach for me and I would greet the people at the end, so they would know I would be there for the next two nights.

I drove through the heavy bumper-to-bumper traffic no longer pressed to get there in time and began worshipping the Lord in my car. As I was worshipping, I felt lighter and lighter and about 45 minutes into the heavenly worship, I suddenly found myself at the exit that would take me to the church. I ended up at the church only 45 minutes later at 8:15 p.m. I was confused thinking maybe I had miscalculated what time it was.

I walked in and the pastor was still leading the worship, he almost passed out when he saw me walk in. He ran up to me asking me if I took a helicopter. He explained to me there was no humanly way possible with bumper-to-bumper traffic on a Friday night from Paris that I made a three-hour drive in 45 minutes. I realized at that point I had been supernaturally transported. I still had to drive the entire three hours back after the meetings, though. I realized God really wanted me in that meeting for the unsaved souls who would need to be saved and healed that night.

These type of experiences have occurred several times. Another time we had an eight-hour drive from the northwest of France to the farthest northeast town. The same thing happened as Stephanie and I and the driver were worshipping for about one and one-half hours while driving, when suddenly we were at the turn and at the church. God wanted us to not miss the meeting that night.

Yet another time in New Zealand on the way to a revival meeting, a flock of sheep blocked the windy, rural road. We honked and were stuck for quite a while until finally a sheepdog appeared barking and scaring the sheep to move along. At this point we were super late and would have missed the meeting. We had another hour to drive, yet somehow we were there in 15 minutes.

Over and over we have seen this occur and I am still dumbfounded, humbled, and in awe that this still happens in our modern day.

We need to expect that in the end times as God speeds up His harvest and increases His Glory, that being transported will become more and more common in these last days to speed up the harvest!

Why Crossing Borders Increases the Power of God

Mark 16:15 (NIV) says, "*He said to them, 'Go into all the world and preach the gospel to all creation.'*"

God commands us to go into all the world and preach the gospel! When we obey and go into all the world to share the gospel, we are automatically promised that we will see the power of God. What does God promise when we go into all the world, cross borders, nations and territories? The Bible tells us in Mark 16:17-18 (NIV):

> *And* ***these signs will accompany those who believe:*** *In my name they will drive out demons; they will speak in new tongues; they will pick up snakes with their hands; and when they drink deadly poison, it will not hurt them at all; they will place their hands on sick people, and they will get well.*

Have you ever noticed that if you go on a missions trip with your church and you pray for people, it seems as if miracles, healings, and deliverances flow effortlessly, as well as people getting saved? This is as opposed to doing the same in your home church or in your own town with people that know you? It still occurs but seemingly at a slower pace.

The promise of the power of God manifesting with the sharing of the gospel outside your own town or your own area is right there in the Scriptures. Then the more you do it or even go to other areas near your town and you see the power of God and souls saved, it gives you greater faith and increases the glory on your life to return to your own area and see more people healed and saved. It does not matter if you are not evangelistically inclined, the Bible says these signs will follow all who believe (Mark 16:17). The sharing of our faith and preaching the gospel is for every believer to do in our respective spheres of influence and communities, as well as going outside our own towns to reach others.

Feeding the Poor Evangelism

I believe that in the near future, some cities will be so devastated with natural or man-made disasters and economic crashes they will lack basic necessities, including food, water, and medicine; local governments will not have the capacity to take care of all their own citizens as the need will be overwhelming. This is where the church can shine and harvest the most fertile fields of the unsaved masses! Most ministries usually focus on one or the other—wining souls or humanitarian aid. Both of which are commanded by the Bible to do. But when you fuse these two together, there will be a quantum leap of harvest as we have never seen! I believe soon this will become the model for many ministers who are trying to reach the lost or reach their city and nations in these last days!

We already know from reading the Bible that there will be famines, pestilence, wars, and natural disasters on a much greater scale; so we know in advance there will be need for water, food, medicine, shelters, and healing ministries due to these situations. What if we prepared in advance for these events, to be proactive instead of reactive, to be ready in season or out of season for any and every opportunity to reach the masses. Our churches need to take advantage of every opportunity to share the gospel, including times when people are in great need.

The Key to Unlocking World Harvest

When I was a young missionary living in Paris, France, God gave me a fresh revelation while on a three-day fast. I began to read the book of Romans.

My spiritual eyes were opened at a very young age to the mystery of the end-time harvest that even some of the most-known evangelistic ministries seemed to have overlooked in their endeavors for world evangelism.

Romans 11:13-15 (NLT) says:

> *I am saying all this especially for you Gentiles. God has appointed me as the apostle to the Gentiles. I stress this, for I want somehow to make the people of Israel jealous of what you Gentiles have, so I might save some of them. For since their rejection meant that God*

> *offered salvation to the rest of the world, their acceptance will be even more wonderful. It will be life for those who were dead!*

This passage was the key I was looking for! France is an extremely unreached nation with less than 1 percent Christians. When sharing the gospel there, it seemed like people were not interested in knowing Jesus. So I needed the right key to unlock this nation. The Lord began to show me that the end-time harvest is connected to Israel being saved. As more Jews in Israel come to salvation, it unleashes a multiplication factor worldwide. Whatever happens to Israel happens worldwide. The Lord began to show me clearly how the end-time harvest will speed up.

When the disciples asked Jesus when He would return to planet Earth and to Israel after He departs, His answer was recorded in Matthew 23:39 (NIV), *"For I tell you, you will not see me again until you say, 'Blessed is he who comes in the name of the Lord.'"*

This means that when a certain remnant of saved Jewish people are calling Him back and blessing Him, Yeshua, the Messiah, will return.

So Jesus is in Heaven waiting until there is a remnant number of Jews in Israel who have to be saved and call Him back. This in turn causes a worldwide harvest as well to accelerate. As the born-again remnant in Israel grows, this causes a boomerang effect as the worldwide harvest starts to speed up dramatically! So think of it this way. Jesus is in Heaven looking at Israel and sees the number of Jews being saved, this then speeds up the worldwide harvest among the Gentile nations, which in turn makes the Jews even more jealous to know their Messiah, which in turn speeds up His return.

We cannot get the remaining holdout nations radically saved, such as North Korea, Saudi Arabia, and other virtually untouched nations with the gospel, and Jesus cannot come back until a certain remnant of Jews are saved in Israel calling Him back! Most people think the Jews in Israel will only be saved when Jesus returns, and they will mourn for the One whom they pierced. That is partly true, but there are two parts to the Israeli harvest. There is the one occurring now, and the remnant there being saved is mostly the poor, new immigrants from Eastern Europe and Russia, as well as from Ethiopia and secular Israelis. Then there are some religious and rabbis being saved in secret and waiting before they can share it publicly.

But for the most part the religious leaders and those in authority in Israel will be saved once He returns the second time and they see Him for who He is. But the first revival occurring now leading up to and after the war of Gog and Magog and Armageddon, which I referenced earlier, speeds up the end-time harvest leading to His return.

In the 1960s during the Jesus Movement when many of the hippies got saved, more Jews were saved during that time than any other time since the time of Jesus. Before that period, there were only a handful of messianic congregations in Israel. After that, the number skyrocketed both in Israel and the USA.

Paul said he was called to go to the Gentiles primarily. His strategy was to go to the Jew first, that's why he said, *"I magnify my ministry"* by going to the Jew first (Romans 11:13 NKJV). That also follows the protocol for world harvest.

Romans 1:16 (NKJV), *"For I am not ashamed of the gospel of Christ, for it is the power of God to salvation for everyone who believes, for the Jew first and also for the Greek."*

So I realized if I would reach Israel first with my own ministry with both salvation and humanitarian needs like helping the poor in Israel, my ministry would start to be extremely fruitful, exponentially more than if I did not follow that mandate.

So shortly after that time of fasting and praying, I signed up to go to Israel with our Bible school where I had graduated from in Dallas, Texas (CFNI). We needed $3,000 and that was all the money we had, having just sold my car in the USA for that exact amount. The Lord told us to go and win souls.

On the three-week tour and outreach, I led 13 Israelis to the Lord. Ten were Jewish and the other three were Arab Israelis. When I returned to France, suddenly I was in a period of revival for five straight years, from 1993-1998. Every week revival meetings with healings, miracles, and salvations were occurring in churches all over France and the French-speaking world where I was ministering, including France, Belgium, French-speaking Switzerland, Luxembourg, French Caribbean islands including Martinique, Guadeloupe, and Saint Martin, and in Africa in Madagascar, Ivory Coast, and Gabon as well as in French Guyana in South America. The fifth year ended with the longest-running revival in 50 years in a church in France. It was six months straight of new souls saved in every service, believers and non-believers repenting of sin by bringing articles of sin to the altar, and remarkable miracles and deliverances occurring.

Then in 1999, God told me to bless Israel again and plan to go to Israel, but this time by ourselves without a tour. We bought tickets not knowing what we would do there. Then doors opened to speak in Jerusalem at both Ruth Heflin's meetings and also in the old city at one of the oldest churches there. And the third was in Herzliya near Tel Aviv. In all of these meetings there were amazing miracles and signs and wonders and salvations.

When we returned to France, God opened even more great and mighty doors! Suddenly we were renting out large civic centers where only the most famous American evangelists would preach once every few years. Yet we were renting these places every three months! And to top it off, a Dutch ministry offered to air our civic center meetings on their *TBN Europe* prime time slot every Sunday night for free as long as they could film our meetings with their professional crew and sell the videos to those attending.

God suddenly catapulted our ministry and effectiveness and multiplied greatly the number of people we were reaching in France, all over Europe, and the French-speaking world! Doors started to fly open all over Europe and the nations! I believe and know 100 percent that a primary reason for this—apart from stepping out in faith to do these things—was blessing Israel first! We continued to give to ministries in Israel that were reaching the lost and feeding the poor. We have not stopped to this day.

In 2024 we saw the largest number of souls saved in Israel in a single meeting, and the same year saw the largest number of souls saved in just one trip to Pakistan. We also started a humanitarian organization in Israel in 2020. We have been sending many thousands of dollars every month since the pandemic and continue to this day to help the poorest and most needy who cannot even put food on the table in Israel. This is a promise in the Bible for blessing also. Jesus says in Matthew 25:40 (NKJV), *"And the King will answer and say to them, 'Assuredly, I say to you, inasmuch as you did it to one of the least of these My brethren, you did it to Me.'"*

When Jesus said the least of these *"My brethren,"* He is talking about the people of Israel first, the poorest of His own people in the flesh. The gospel is to the Jew first because they were the first to receive the gospel and to spread it to the Gentile world. Now it's our turn to bring it back to them. As the gospel is to the Jew first, just as the Jews were the firstborn to bring Gentiles the gospel; so at the end of the book of Malachi, God says He will turn the hearts of the children back to the fathers and the fathers to the children. The spiritual forefathers of the church were the Jewish apostles, and the church is now turning their hearts to pray for Israel and the Jewish people for whom we owe much—and many in Israel are turning their hearts back to the church and Christians, realizing we love them and stand with them in these intense times.

Here is another interesting passage in Luke 7:3-6 (NIV):

> *The centurion heard of Jesus and sent some elders of the Jews to him, asking him to come and heal his servant. When they came to Jesus, they pleaded earnestly with him, "This man deserves to have you do this, because he loves our nation and has built our synagogue." So Jesus went with them....*

Notice Jesus did not say no or that helping the Jewish people in having a place to worship does not make a difference. Instead, after hearing that the servant had helped and loved the Jewish people, Jesus prayed for the centurion's servant to be healed, and he was healed from a distance. There is a blessing in blessing Israel and the Jewish people, whether it be spiritually with the gospel or naturally with helping them.

Why the Jews Have Priority

The Jews have a priority over Gentiles as the chosen people of God to hear the gospel first.

Why do they have priority over Gentiles? In Genesis 12, God chose Abraham and his descendants freely from all the peoples of the world to bless with His covenant and promise. Consider these biblical passages:

- Nehemiah 9:7 (NIV) says, "*You are the Lord God who chose Abram and brought him out from Ur of the Chaldees and named him Abraham.*"
- Deuteronomy 14:2 (NKJV) says about the Jewish people as a whole, "*...the Lord has chosen you to be a people for Himself, a special treasure above all the peoples who are on the face of the earth.*"
- Amos 3:2 (NIV) says, "*You only have I chosen of all the families of the earth....*"
- Romans 11:28-29 (AMP) says, "*From the standpoint of the gospel, the Jews [at present] are enemies [of God] for your sake [which is for your benefit], but from the standpoint of God's choice [of the Jews as His people], they are still loved by Him for the sake of the fathers. For the gifts and the calling of God are irrevocable....*"

1. The Jews have a priority over Greeks (that is, all Gentiles, by implication) because of their special role as God's elect or chosen people.

He set His favor on them and set them apart from all the peoples. Freely! Not because of any virtue or special value in them, but simply on the basis of His free choice: "*The Lord did not set His love on you nor choose you because you were more in number than any other people, for you were the least of all peoples; but because the Lord loves you, and because He would keep the oath which He swore to your fathers...*" (Deuteronomy 7:7-8 NKJV).

2. The Jews have a priority over Gentiles as the guardians of God's special revelation as told in the Old Testament Scriptures.

In Romans 3:1 (NASB), Paul asks our question: "*Then what advantage does the Jew have? Or what is the benefit of circumcision?*" And he answers in verse 2, "*Great in every respect. First, that they were entrusted with the actual words of God.*" So, God gave his special revelation and promises to Israel by Moses and the prophets. Romans 9:4 (NASB) puts it like this: "[They] *are Israelites to whom belongs...the covenants, the giving of the Law...and the promises.*"

All the great expressions and foreshadowings of the gospel of salvation were given to the Jews in the Word of God, the Old Testament. So the Jews had priority in having the Scriptures.

3. The Jews have a priority over the Gentiles in that the Messiah Himself, Jesus Christ, came first as a Jew to the Jews.

In Romans 9:5, Paul brings his list of privileges to a climax with these words: "*From* [the Jews] *is the Christ according to the flesh, who is over all, God blessed forever. Amen.*" The Messiah, Jesus, is a Jew, born of the seed of David (Romans 1:3 NKJV). And He focused His earthly ministry on the Jews—they had priority in His work.

In Matthew 10:5-6 (NKJV) Jesus says to the twelve apostles as He sent them out, "*Do not go into the way of the Gentiles, and do not enter a city of the Samaritans. But go rather to the lost sheep of the house of Israel.*" And in Matthew 15:24 (NIV), Jesus says, "*I was sent only to the lost sheep of Israel.*" So during His earthly life, Jesus was focused on the Jews. They had priority in His ministry.

4. The Jews have a priority over the Gentiles in that salvation is from the Jews.

These are the very words of Jesus in John 4:22 (NIV): Jesus says to the woman at the well, "*You Samaritans worship what you do not know; we* [Jews] *worship what we know, for salvation is from the Jews.*" This simply sums up all that we have seen so far. The Jews are the chosen nation; the nation with God's special revelation; and the nation with the Messiah, the Savior. So, clearly, salvation is "*from the Jews.*"

Another way to see that salvation is from the Jews is found in Romans 11:17-24 where Paul compares the Jewish nation to an olive tree. He says that natural branches are broken off and unnatural branches were grafted in, meaning that Jews by birth were unbelieving and so cut off from the covenant of promise for a season; and Gentiles who were believing were grafted in and saved by the covenant of promise.

Romans 11:17-18 (NIV) are crucial for us to understand: "*If some of the branches have been broken off, and you, though a wild olive shoot, have been grafted in among the others and now share in the nourishing sap from the olive root, do not consider yourself to be superior to those other branches. If you do, consider this: You do not support the root, but the root supports you.*"

In other words, salvation comes to us Gentiles from the root of God's covenant with the Jews.

We are simply grafted in like wild olive branches that have no historical claim at all on being God's people. And God saves us by reckoning us as children of Abraham by faith, as Paul says in Galatians 3:7 (NIV), *"Understand, then, that those who have faith are children of Abraham."*

So Jews have priority because *"salvation is from the Jews."* All salvation is salvation through God's covenant with Abraham!

5. The Jews have a priority over the Gentiles in that Paul evangelized Jews first when he brought the gospel to a new place.

For example, in Acts 13:46 (NIV) Paul and Barnabas are preaching in Antioch of Pisidia, and the Jews will not listen to the gospel, so they say, *"We had to speak the word of God to you first. Since you reject it and do not consider yourselves worthy of eternal life, we now turn to the Gentiles."* In other words, just as God chose Israel and revealed Himself to Israel and sent the Messiah and Savior to Israel so that salvation is from Israel, it is fitting that in the spread of the gospel to new places, the Jews hear first of their Messiah and the good news of His salvation. So Jews have a priority in the order of frontier missions when the gospel is introduced to the people in a new place.

6. The Jews have a priority over the Gentiles in final judgment and final blessing.

In Romans 2:9-10 (NIV), Paul says, amazingly, *"There will be trouble and distress for every human being who does evil: first for the Jew, then for the Gentile; but glory, honor and peace for everyone who does good: first for the Jew, then for the Gentile."* In other words, the priority that the Jews have, if it is rejected and squandered will result in a priority in judgment. And if they are grateful for their priority and trust in the mercy of their Messiah, then they will go first into the final blessing of God. There are definite dangers in having this priority including: "*From everyone who has been given much, much will be demanded; and from the one who has been entrusted with much, much more will be asked*" (Luke 12:48 NIV).

So when Paul says in Romans 1:16 (NASB), "*the gospel...is the power of God for salvation to everyone who believes, to the Jew first and also to the Greek,*" we should call to mind these six ways that the Jews have a priority over the Gentiles:

1. The Jews are the historic chosen people of God.
2. They are the guardians of God's special revelation, the Old Testament Scriptures.
3. The Messiah and Savior, Jesus, comes to the world as a Jew to Jews.
4. Salvation is from the Jews, since everyone who is saved is saved by being connected to the covenant with Abraham by faith.
5. The Jews are to be evangelized first when the gospel penetrates a new region.
6. The Jews will enter first into final judgment and final blessing.

In What Ways Do the Jews *Not* Have Priority?

Now before we ask why Paul says this and what effect it should have on us, let's be sure we see several ways that the Jews do *not* have priority. This understanding is extremely important.

1. The Jews do not have priority in righteousness or merit.

Nor do Gentiles. We are on the same footing. That is one of the main points of the first two chapters of Romans. Paul concludes in Romans 3:9-10 (NASB), "*What then? Are we* [Jews] *better than they* [Gentiles]? *Not at all; for we have already charged that both Jews and Greeks are all under sin; as it is written, 'There is no righteous person, not even one.'*" He makes the same point in Romans 3:22-23 (NASB), "*...there is no distinction; for all have sinned and fall short of the glory of God.*"

2. The Jews do not have priority in how they are saved.

The Jews are saved exactly the way Gentiles are saved. This is clear from Romans 3:29-30 (NASB), "*Is God the God of Jews only? Is He not the God of Gentiles also? Yes, of Gentiles also...God who will justify the circumcised by faith and the uncircumcised through faith.*" And from Romans 10:12-13 (NASB), "*There is no distinction between Jew and Greek; for the same Lord is Lord of all, abounding in riches for all who call on Him; for 'Everyone who calls on the name of the Lord will be saved.'*" So neither Jews nor Gentiles have priority in how they are saved—both are saved by faith in Christ, not in any ethnic or religious distinctive.

3. The Jews do not have priority in participation in God's covenant blessings.

The mystery of the gospel that Paul preaches, he says, is that Gentiles are now full partners in the blessings of Jewish salvation. Consider Ephesians 2:12-13 and 18-19 (NASB), "*Remember that you* [Gentiles] *were at that time separate from Christ* [the Messiah], *excluded from the people of Israel, and strangers to the covenants of the promise, having no hope and without God in the world. But now in Christ Jesus you who previously were far away have been brought near by the blood of Christ. ...through Him we both have our access in one Spirit to the Father. So then you are no longer strangers and foreigners, but you are fellow citizens with the saints, and are of God's household.*" Again in Ephesians 3:4-6 (NASB), "*...when you read you can understand my insight into the mystery of Christ that the Gentiles are fellow heirs and fellow members of the body, and fellow partakers of the promise in Christ Jesus* [the Messiah Jesus] *through the gospel.*"

So Jews do not have priority in participation in God's covenant blessings. Gentiles are full heirs of all the promises of God.

Why Did Paul Mention the Priority of the Jews?

So we come to a close with the question: Why did Paul mention this priority of the Jews in Romans 1:16 (NASB) writing, "*For I am not ashamed of the gospel, for it is the power of God for salvation to everyone who believes, to the Jew first and also to the Greek*"? What effect should it have?

Being influenced by Romans 11:17-32, I think the answer is that Paul wants to humble both Jew and Greek and make them deeply aware that they depend entirely on mercy, not on themselves or their tradition or ethnic connections. To the Gentiles he says, in essence, salvation is of the Jews. You are not being saved by your Greek culture—or any other culture. You are being saved by a salvation that comes through the despised Semitic people called the Jews: *"You do not support the root* [of the Abrahamic covenant], *the root supports you."* So do not boast over the branches (Romans 11:18). We Gentiles are saved by becoming, as it were, spiritual Jews (Romans 2:28-29). This should humble us and strip us of any arrogance and boasting in any presumed ethnic superiority. It also should vanquish anti-Semitism and fill us with zeal for evangelism to Jews.

Similarly, Paul says to the Jews, your salvation is not your own. It is God's and He gives it to whom He pleases. He can raise up from stones—even Gentile stones!—children to Abraham (Matthew 3:9). The words *"also to the Greek"* in Romans 1:16 would have been as offensive to the Jews as the words *"to the Jew first"* were to the Gentiles. What they thought were Jewish prerogatives are, in fact, shared by the lowliest Gentiles who believe.

Both are being humbled. Gentiles must humble themselves to be saved through a Jewish Messiah and a Jewish covenant. Jews must humble themselves to receive formerly "unclean" Gentiles into full covenant relationship and share all the blessings of the promise of Abraham.

The whole point is that God is the One who has mercy. Ethnicity is not decisive here. There is no merit with Him. We are all sinners. So the real emphasis falls back on that wonderful word "everyone" that we started with: *"The gospel is the power of God to* ***everyone*** *who believes."* So, whether Jew or Gentile, believe! And receive the power of God to save you from your sins and guilt and death and judgment and hell, and bring you home to ever-increasing joy in His presence forever and ever.

In the next verse, Ezekiel has a vision of the third temple and the glory of the Lord filled the temple as God says never again will humankind defile His land or temple.

> *Then I heard Him* [God] *speaking to me from the temple, **while a man*** [Jesus] ***stood beside me.** And He said to me, "Son of man, this is the place of My throne and the place of the soles of My feet, where I will dwell in the midst of the children of Israel forever. No more shall the house of Israel defile My holy name, they nor their kings, by their harlotry or with the carcasses of their kings on their high places. When they set their threshold by My threshold, and their doorpost by My doorpost, with a wall between them and Me, they defiled My holy name by the abominations which they committed; therefore I have consumed them in My anger. Now let them put their harlotry and the carcasses of their kings far away from Me, and I will dwell in their midst forever"* (Ezekiel 43:6-9 NKJV).

God the Father is clearly speaking to the prophet from His seated throne on earth that He will dwell with the children of Israel in the final temple. The man standing next to Ezekiel was Jesus, as we know Jesus is always next to the Father and in Heaven on the throne, so likewise He would be there next to Him on earth! The Father came before—He will come again with Jesus.

11

END-TIME TIMELINE—WHAT'S COMING?

So now we find ourselves in the beginning of the very end times.

We are also in the time of sorrow and birth pangs. These are times of intensity, pressure, chaos in the world—but at the same time there is a great harvest of souls and a great demonstration of the power of God in these last days!

We are living in the final generation that the apostles and prophets of old foresaw and wished they could see in their day—but here we are!

So to know what is coming and where we are on the end-time timeline, we have to first look at the fig tree, which is Israel, to see how ripe it is.

The fig tree prophecy references part of Jesus' Olivet Discourse recorded in Matthew 24, Mark 13, and Luke 21.

The following is what Jesus says:

> *Now learn this lesson from the fig tree: As soon as its twigs get tender and its leaves come out, you know that summer is near. Even so, when you see all these things, you know that it is near, right at the door. Truly I tell you, this generation will certainly not pass away until all these things have happened. Heaven and earth*

> *will pass away, but my words will never pass away* (Matthew 24:32-35 NIV).

Fig trees were common in Israel, so Jesus used this illustration of a sign of the end times. The appearance of leaves on the fig tree heralded the onset of summer; similarly, the appearance of all the things Jesus had just described would herald the Second Coming and the end of the age.

Note the wording of the fig tree prophecy: Jesus says that when people see all the signs, then the end is near. What are all the signs? The following is what Jesus has mentioned in Matthew 24:5-30) up to that point:

- Many false messiahs will come (Matthew 24:5)
- There will be wars and rumors of wars (verse 6)
- Nations will rise against each other (verse 7)
- There will be famines and earthquakes worldwide (verse 7)
- Christians will face persecution and death (verse 9)
- Many professed believers will turn away from the faith and betray each other (verse 10)
- Many false prophets will deceive masses of people (verses 11, 24)
- Wickedness will increase (verse 12)
- The love of most will grow cold (verse 12)
- The gospel will be preached to the whole world (verse 14)
- The abomination of desolation will stand in the holy place of the temple (verse 15; Daniel 9:27)
- There will be a time of great distress, unequaled in the history of the world (verse 21)
- There will be signs in the heavens affecting the sun, moon, and stars (verse 29)
- The sign of the Son of Man will appear in Heaven (verse 30)

According to the fig tree prophecy, *"when you see all these things, you can know his return is very near, right at the door"* (Matthew 24:33 NLT). There were some present when Jesus spoke this who had seen some of the things Jesus prophesied (false teachers and persecution, for example), but His return will not occur until *all* are seen in fullness. We consider the events Jesus lists as corresponding to the seal judgments of Revelation 6.

Jesus goes on to say, *"Truly I tell you, this generation will certainly not pass away until all these things have happened"* (Matthew 24:34 NIV). The generation that Jesus speaks of not passing until He returns is a future generation, namely, the people living when the predicted events occur. They are the people alive in the future when all the events of Matthew chapters 24–25 take place.

In other words, the people who will see the start of those events will be the same people who see the end of those events. As one scholar puts it, "The generation that sees the beginning of the end, also sees its end. When the signs come, they will proceed quickly; they will not drag on for many generations. It will happen within a generation."[8]

This sequence of events hasn't fully happened yet. To use Jesus' illustration, the leaves of the fig tree have not yet emerged. When they do, the world can know that Jesus is coming soon. The fig tree prophecy concerns His Second Coming. The Second Coming is preceded by signs, just as summer is preceded by the fig leaves.

Also, we don't know when the events of Matthew 24 will occur. *"About that day or hour no one knows,"* Jesus says in Matthew 24:36 (NIV). So we don't know 100 percent if anyone alive today will see all these signs, but it sure is looking like it every day as things are rapidly speeding up. We believe we are getting closer to that time—we certainly aren't getting farther away—and we pray, *"Thy kingdom come"* (Matthew 6:10 KJV). As we wait and pray and observe the *"birth pains"* (Matthew 24:8 NIV), we remember the fig tree prophecy.

But just because we don't know the day or the hour, we *can* possibly know the season. Most of the major events of Jesus all occurred during a Hebrew feast that God gave to Israel. Most Jewish scholars believe He was conceived at Hannukah, which is the feast of dedication. He died at Passover and was the Passover Lamb! The Holy Spirit was sent on the Hebrew feast of Pentecost! And one of the last unfulfilled feasts is the Feast of Tabernacles. It starts off with the fall Feasts, which starts with Rosh Hashanah leading to Yom Kippur—but primarily the Feast of Tabernacles. It's very possible Jesus returns during a Yom Kippur when the entire nation is fasting and mourning, which is what occurs on that day, but they will be repenting and mourning for the One whom they pierced.

Zechariah 12:10-14 (NIV) says:

> *And I will pour out on the house of David and the inhabitants of Jerusalem a spirit of grace and supplication. They will look on me, the one they have pierced, and they will mourn for him as one mourns for an only child, and grieve bitterly for him as one grieves for a firstborn son. On that day the weeping in Jerusalem will be as great as the weeping of Hadad Rimmon in the plain of Megiddo. The land will mourn, each clan by itself, with their wives by themselves: the clan of the house of David and their wives, the clan of the house of Nathan and their wives, the clan of the house of Levi and their wives, the clan of Shimei and their wives, and all the rest of the clans and their wives.*

Just two chapters later it's the Feast of Tabernacles. It seems very possible there is national mourning for having missed the Messiah when He first came and realizing He is the Messiah after all. This realization will hit the spiritual, religious, and national leaders in full. Then shortly after this and He has returned, it will be a Feast of Tabernacles unlike any other!

The Feast of Tabernacles is already known as the most joyful feast, but when the Messiah appears it will be fully fulfilled. Every nation will be required to go to Jerusalem during this feast to worship the King, Yeshua/Jesus including the Arab nations. That's how we know the feasts are not just ancient celebrations or only for the Jewish people today. The Feast of Tabernacles is also called the feast of all nations. Now we see why. All nations will come during that time to worship Him or at least send representatives from their respective nations. Look what it says here just two chapters after the mourning:

> *And it shall come to pass that everyone who is left of all the nations which came against Jerusalem shall go up from year to year to worship the King, the Lord of hosts, and to keep the Feast of Tabernacles. And it shall be that whichever of the families of the earth do not come up to Jerusalem to worship the King, the Lord of hosts, on them there will be no rain. If the family of Egypt will not come up and enter in, they shall have no rain; they shall receive the plague with which the Lord strikes the nations who do not come up to keep the Feast of Tabernacles. This shall be the punishment of Egypt and the punishment of all the nations that do not come up to keep the Feast of Tabernacles* (Zechariah 14:16-19 NKJV).

On a side note, if there is a blessing of rain for going and celebrating the Feast of Tabernacles in Jerusalem while King Yeshua/Jesus is present, could there be a blessing in blessing Israel today during those feasts while awaiting and preparing for His return? I did an experiment and went to Israel during this feast with a tour of believers to pray, visit, and bless Israel. During that trip I was offered a contract for a TV show, television cameras were given to me by another ministry, and international doors opened—all before I left Israel. A "rain" of favor surely hit our ministry during that time.

Events That Must Still Occur

As I wrote earlier, it looks like the Psalm 83 wars are still in process as Israel is fighting to protect its nation from the bordering nations. The next big war after this seems to be the Gog and Magog war. For this to occur, nations that have never been aligned must join alliances against Israel. The main nations involved would be Russia, Iran, and Turkey, and other nations will tag along. The Bible says that God puts a hook in the jaw of Russia. What is amazing is that these nations have never been aligned, and Russia and Turkey have been at great odds in the past with each other. Yet for the first time in history these nations will form economic and military alliances.

So what is the hook in the jaw causing Russia to attack Israel with the others? Iran! (And newly discovered huge oil and natural gas reserves in Israel.) Also important to note concerning the Gog and Magog war is that people think it's mostly Russia because Rosh sounds like Russia, but it's not. *Rosh* means head or chief, like in Rosh Hashanah, head of the year; it's not a place but a title. The area is Meshech and Tubal.

Meshec and Tubal are in Turkey. This area's leadership attitude toward Israel makes sense as they have been threatening Israel constantly, upset that Israel has taken the other half of the Golan Heights. Turkey once controlled Jerusalem, but in World War II they allied with Germany and Hitler. When Germany lost the war, the allies took over and released Israel from Turkey's control. Turkey wants to take back all the nations it conquered, including Israel and Jerusalem especially. Turkey very well may be the main instigator setting up the Gog and Magog war. Russia, still involved through its alliance with Iran, will also join in.

Ezekiel 39:6 says, "*I will send fire on Magog and on those who live in security in the coastlands. Then they shall know that I am the* Lord." The Gog and Magog war could happen before the tribulation period during a time of peace and prosperity with Israel dwelling securely, as the Bible points out the conditions prior to the war.

Russia also has signed a military treaty with Iran that if either nation is attacked the other must come to the rescue. Russia is already depleting its military with the war in Ukraine and would be reluctant to go to another war now. But with Iran supplying drones and other things Russia wants, and to keep this treaty and not lose face, it may reluctantly feel obliged to help Iran in attacking Israel.

Now what would cause such a need for Iran to try to get other nations to join in? The reason is that Iran on its own cannot defeat Israel. Already, as of this writing, Iran's capabilities have been greatly diminished by Israel directly, and Israel has degraded Iran's proxies in Gaza, Lebanon, Syria, and Yemen.

Iran still has some nuclear capabilities left, and most likely, Israel (possibly with the USA) will knock out those capabilities, leaving it totally vulnerable as its economy will have also been destroyed and its ability to help Russia with drones and other equipment will cease. This would infuriate Iran and the treaty with Russia would pull Russia in, reluctantly, after Iran regroups from being further diminished militarily by Israel. Also, Israel will be flowing in natural gas and oil that Russia was once the leader of, making lots of money selling to Europe, which could also draw Russia in for some loot as it loses sales of its resources, while Israel rises more and more economically.

Turkey is one the nations mentioned and plays a major role, as it has the largest army in Europe, although most of its territory is in Asia. Also, in 2024, the rebels who took down the leader of Syria, Assad, was completely backed by Turkey. So much so that Israel is now contemplating that Turkey in essence could already be on its border via the proxy of the new government in Syria that was a former member of al-Qaeda; many of them were parading ISIS flags as they took over Damascus, the capital of Syria.

So what would draw Turkey into the war? Well, we have yet to see the capital of Syria utterly destroyed in one hour as the Bible predicts. And if Syria is now really a proxy of Turkey, then this would easily be the trigger for Turkey to go fully to war with Israel joining Russia and Iran along with a confederacy of other nations. (Possibly European nations that have a common interest in attacking Israel.)

Now after such a "Great War" that Israel again wins thanks to the God of Israel Himself coming out this time to defend Israel directly, as no other nations comes to Israel's rescue as in the Gog and Magog war, what would Israel do next?

The Third Temple

The most pivotal end-time event to understand upon which all the other worldwide events revolve is the building of the third temple in Jerusalem. Also, God seems to follow His ancient patterns in using a Cyrus-type of figure to help Israel.

President Donald Trump is often referred to as a modern-day Cyrus. He declared Jerusalem the undivided capital of the Jewish people and moved the US embassy to Jerusalem, which no other president dared to do. I actually prophesied this one hour before Trump was to be inaugurated just a few blocks away at the 2016 inauguration. I was attending the Prayer Breakfast held at the Trump Hotel in DC. I also prophesied that to Make America Great Again it would depend on the US standing with Israel in a greater way.

Among the people attending the Prayer Breakfast in 2016 were Knesset members, politicians, pastors and leaders and believers on the morning of the inauguration. The Israeli officials came up to me in tears thanking me for the word and gave me a picture book about Jerusalem signed to President Donald Trump; they thought he might be at the event but could not so they handed it to me. About 11 months later, President Trump moved the US embassy to Jerusalem.

The word I also received was that the main reason God allowed President Trump into power was to stand with Israel and help her accomplish her purposes and declare Jerusalem the capital. I believe the reason God allowed him to have a second term as far as Heaven's end-time perspective goes, is so the USA will continue to stand with Israel and bring a season of peace to Israel in the region, which will pave the way for Israel's rebuilding of the third temple.

I actually had a very clear dream about this recently while on a fast up in the mountains in a cabin. In the dream I asked President Trump if he was involved in any way in the third temple. In the dream he looked at me very surprised that I knew this, as there was no news anywhere about it. He said to me yes, in fact he was talking and working behind the scenes to help create the framework for Israel to achieve this reality. I woke up with such a surprise and a strong feeling of the shortness of the hour and time in which we live.

I believe President Trump, in his second term, will be used to stop the attacks on Israel coming from all sides—starting with Iran and its proxies in Gaza, Lebanon, Syria, Iraq, and Yemen—giving Israel cover. President Trump will pave the way for a season of peace and prosperity unlike anything Israel has seen.

Of course the peace will be a false peace and last possibly only a few years during President Trump's second term. But God can do great things during this breather time in history and believers can seize the moment and win as many souls as possible during this false peace.

Along with false peace come false messiahs, false prophets, and even possibly a false currency economic system, comprising of digits on a screen and even no longer using paper money.

Huge opportunities such as crypto currency and AI technologies will be in the forefront of the US and the Western monetary system. In the short term, this will be a blessing and some believers who see what is occurring can profit, making huge gains when it reaches a peak. People will convert those assets to paying off debt, buying land, farms, gold, silver, building Goshens (cities of prosperity, favor and divine protection), and especially using these funds for the advancement of the gospel and for safe palaces for God's people in these end times!

Just as Joseph experienced years of plenty then years of famine in Egypt, he knew when to store during the good times to prepare for the hard times, which made Egypt the world power at the time due to Joseph's wisdom and foreseeing the future. God can do the same for His people who can discern the timings and seasons they are in at any given moment.

This will be an interim period of being blessed, but future governments will use this same digital tokenized currency and blockchain technology powered by a new super AI to control the world financially, giving everyone a number and a mark most likely stored on a final blockchain technology powered by a powerful AI that can handle the world's data in a millisecond.

You have to know what season in history you are in and also in the financial world to know what to do. But to those who can see what's ahead, they can maximize the moment with the relative peace coming for a very short time and plan ahead for when the false peace ends.

During this season of peace and prosperity, the Abraham Accords will be increasing with even nations like Saudi Arabia. It seems this second treaty expanding peace may require sharing the Temple Mount by Jews and Muslims with both the third temple and the Dome of the Rock mosque there together, or at least agree to it in theory. At some point Israel will be allowed and even be encouraged to go ahead build the third temple, especially when Saudi Arabia joins in.

Just as Cyrus, the head of the largest world power of his day helped Israel build their temple and declare Jerusalem and Israel as belonging to them, so could it be that President Trump is destined to bring peace and stability to Israel and the region, paving the way for them to eventually build the third temple. It's technically possible that we could start to see the very beginnings of the building yet still not be in that seven-year, end-time period depending on how long it will take to build it. Especially depending if they have to start and stop due to world events. We only know that once it's built that the end-time timeline really speeds up.

Many people are confused about the third temple. We know that when they, the Jewish people who are present, start offering animal sacrifices in that third temple, they will eventually realize it's not enough to save them from their sins and that only the blood of the Messiah will suffice. It seems that these events must occur to show Israel that in the end He is the only way, and only His blood will save them. But a temple is supposed to be built and is required for His Second Coming on the timeline. And when it does, world events will revolve around that third temple. For Jesus to return, it's clear there must be a Jewish temple first, according to the Bible, which I will lay out later in this chapter.

During the season of peace and prosperity in Israel, many more Jews will make *aliyah* (immigration to Israel) from the US and Western nations and return to Israel, seeing that it is safe there. Given the anti-Semitism that we see today will continue to explode in the Western nations especially after each of these wars, Israel will be a welcome haven.

Now what happens with the Dome of the Rock on the Temple Mount? There is scriptural evidence to show that both the third temple and the Dome of the Rock will be on the Temple Mount at the same time, most likely as part of a peace deal extending the Abraham Accords in some way. Look what Ezekiel 42:20 (KJV) says:

> *He measured it by the four sides:* ***it had a wall round about,*** *five hundred reeds long, and five hundred broad,*

> *to make a* ***separation*** *between* ***the sanctuary*** *and the* ***profane place.***

The *profane place* seems to be the current Dome of the Rock still standing. It's considered profane as it's a pagan god and structure that Gentiles are worshipping toward Mecca on the Temple Mount.

The area where it is at now was prophesied thousands of years ago in the book of Revelation as John was given a glimpse of end-time events of our day. Revelation mentions the court of the Gentiles way before Gentiles were at the Temple Mount at all; it foresaw the future. Revelation 11:2 (KJV) says, "*But the court which is without the temple leave out, and measure it not; for it is given unto the Gentiles: and the holy city shall they tread under foot forty and two months.*" So an area where the court is without the temple would be the Dome of the Rock; and as we read in Ezekiel 42:20, they make a wall around it to separate it from the temple area.

The key to understand is that the area where the Dome of the Rock is, is the court of the Gentiles area. The third temple will be located where it was originally, which is just to the right of the Dome. When standing on the Mount of Olives looking at the Dome, it would be to the right of it.

Now what is interesting is that this third temple is also the same temple that is defiled by the antichrist. It's not in the Dome of the Rock that he sits in to declare himself god, it is the third temple referred to the "temple of God." It does not say that this temple is bad or the fact that they built it was wrong, but that the man of sin is sitting in "the temple of God" declaring himself god is what profanes it. The Bible refers to it as His temple. Could it be because later when He returns He will also sit in that same temple? Somehow this is His plan all along to show

Himself as the only way, even though He will allow Israel to build the third temple for Him, which I will detail more as you read on.

Second Thessalonians 2:4 (NKJV) states, *"who opposes and exalts himself above all that is called God or that is worshiped, so that he sits as God in* ***the temple of God****, showing himself that he is God."*

So why a third temple before the return of Jesus Christ? Couldn't Christ just decide not to have the third temple built and come back to earth without it?

NO, because otherwise God's end-time prophecy could not be fulfilled! For it is prophesied that there *must* be a third temple before His Second Coming. The Bible gives us numerous impressive prophecies that describe or mention the third temple before Christ's return. Matthew 24:15 refers to the *"abomination of desolation"* in the temple. The New International Version puts it like this: *"So when you see standing in the holy place 'the abomination that causes desolation,' spoken of through the prophet Daniel—let the reader understand…."*

Daniel 11:31 (NIV) reads: *"His armed forces will rise up to desecrate the temple fortress and will abolish the daily sacrifice. Then they will set up the abomination that causes desolation."*

Although some say Antiochus Epiphanes fulfilled this prophecy in his time, this was only a forerunner, because it is an end-time prophecy. It is a prophecy for the third temple. The sacrificing of animals, which according to the Bible is to be taken away, is being prepared in Jerusalem at this present time and will soon reach its climax.

In the second temple there was no mosque or "profane" thing next to it that they had to build a wall to separate it. That would be the Dome of the Rock that is there now and will be known as the court of the Gentiles.

Now is it possible the church is still here during this time or part of this time? This is where the scenario becomes very interesting. Nothing in the Bible clearly says we are not here during this time of the building and even the revealing of the antichrist.

Could we still be here when the temple is being built? Again, that is a yes, as it does not say we are not here. God's Word actually tells us to watch for this event. Also the tribulation and great distress part of the Bible actually occurs in the second half of the seven years, which is the last three and a half years after the antichrist sits in the temple declaring himself God, not before. What does God say about this time?

> *But when ye shall see the abomination of desolation, spoken of by Daniel the prophet, standing where it ought not, (let him that readeth understand,) then let them that be in Judaea flee to the mountains* (Mark 13:14 KJV).

That passage is written to believers and says let him who reads understand. This is talking to believers who read the Word of God. It does not say you won't have to worry about this because you'll be out of here. It gives you signs of the end of the age saying look out for this. When you see.... It does not say if you who backslid or came to the Lord after the rapture and then read this. It's just a continuing passage of signs to watch for.

The Lord gives two keys that signal the return of the Lord. In fact, it warns about being deceived regarding the return of the Lord. Being deceived about this could even lead to a great falling away as people put their guards down. Here are the two key events it says *must* precede the return of the Lord that Paul admonishes believers to watch out for:

> *Let no man deceive you by any means: for that day shall not come, except there come a falling away first, and that man of sin be revealed, the son of perdition* (2 Thessalonians 2:3 KJV).

So one of the deceptions Jesus says in this Scripture verse is in the timing of the day of the return. When Paul says, "*Let no man deceive you,*" he is referring to the fact that some will say Jesus will return before the falling away and before the antichrist is revealed. Could it be that Jesus is telling believers here not to be deceived in thinking He came already, as some were teaching then, or that He will come before the two events he described occurred. These are the two events He tells believers to watch for before His return occurs. If we are not here for this, then why would He tell believers to watch for this.

- Event 1 to watch for: *The great falling away.* So first we need to see the great falling away, which is yet to occur on a grand scale. That means we are still here for this.
- Event 2 to watch for: *The man of sin* (antichrist) *revealed.* This is when he sits in the third temple declaring himself God.

Now we know a great falling away will happen. Could it be that many were taught, like in China before the revolution, that they won't be here for wars, persecution, or even at the building and sitting of the man of sin in the temple? So when these things occur and if possibly we are still here but the great tribulation has not yet started, many could easily fall from the faith saying at this point they are leaving as they don't want to be persecuted or hated by all during this time and didn't sign up for what's coming or were told they would not be here to see any of these things.

Let's be ready and prepared either way and not be so sure we won't be tested during the greatest of these end times. The greatest harvest of souls will occur during the most chaotic and frightening times. We should want to be here as long as possible to win the lost so they too can escape hell and be with Him forever!

God's Wrath Versus Satan's Wrath

The following verses show how end-time believers will win against even the power of the wrath of the antichrist. Revelation 11:11-12 (NLT):

> *And they have defeated him by the blood of the Lamb and by their testimony. And they did not love their lives so much that they were afraid to die. Therefore, rejoice, O heavens! And you who live in the heavens, rejoice! But terror will come on the earth and the sea, for* ***the devil has come down to you in great anger*** [wrath], *knowing that he has little time.*

Many get confused because the Bible says we are not appointed unto God's wrath, thinking that means we are not here for any of the tribulation. And people confuse the wrath of satan with the wrath of God. Satan's wrath during the last three and a half years of tribulation are against those who don't worship him, starting with the Jews but also world. The wrath of God comes at the end of this period against the wicked of the earth. Satan is on a rampage because his time is short to do his work and he tests all on earth to try to punish those who don't worship him.

Revelation 12:12 (AMP) says, "*Therefore rejoice, O heavens, and you who dwell in them [in the presence of God]. Woe to the earth and the sea, because the devil has come down to you in great wrath, knowing that he has only a short time [remaining]!*"

This is clearly the wrath of the devil. He persecutes the saints and all who are of God. This it totally different from God's wrath after that. People assume if we are being persecuted by the antichrist and his system that it's God's wrath or punishment against believers and therefore thinking we cannot be here. Actually the Bible does not say that. It says we will be tested and warns about not following the beast and taking his mark.

The wrath of God toward the end is found here when the last two seals are opened in Heaven. Revelation 6:12-17 (NKJV) tells us:

> *I looked when He opened the sixth seal, and behold, there was a great earthquake; and the sun became black as sackcloth of hair, and the moon became like blood. And the stars of heaven fell to the earth, as a fig tree drops its late figs when it is shaken by a mighty wind. Then the sky receded as a scroll when it is rolled up, and every mountain and island was moved out of its place. And the kings of the earth, the great men, the rich men, the commanders, the mighty men, every slave and every free man, hid themselves in the caves and in the rocks of the mountains, and said to the mountains and rocks, "Fall on us and hide us from the face of*

> *Him who sits on the throne and from the wrath of the Lamb! For the great day of His wrath has come, and who is able to stand?"*

So why am I opening this very intense subject. The main reason is that if we talk about end times, we have to talk about the third temple—the central signpost of the end times, the ultimate red-flag warning that we are in the final countdown. Also knowing that many can and will be deceived, including even the elect of God if He did not shorten those days, I do not want you to be one who is deceived.

Imagine you believe that there is no way we are here when the antichrist first sits in the temple and declares himself God. And let's say you possibly got the timing of the Lord's return and rapture wrong, as no one knows for sure or is 100 percent accurate on all end-time events. But the greater danger is to think you will be out of here before this occurs so you don't have to worry about it. Then let's say there is a new monetary system and you have to get a microchip inserted in your hand or forearm to buy or sell due to the worldwide uncertainty and lawlessness. So in your mind you think, *Well, I need to feed my family and work to live and pay bills. I'm sure God understands.* And then you reason that since the rapture has not occurred yet and believers are still here on earth, this cannot be the antichrist sitting in the temple and this can't be the actual mark of the beast. You may think, *It's just new technology to make things easier and maybe only a precursor to the real one.* Then you could be deceived into taking the mark. This may be especially the thinking of many believers who don't know their Bibles that well and only rely on a sermon in church once a week, if that.

My point is, it's better to err on the side of being ready to live for Him or die for Him at any point, knowing that in the Bible it says we will be persecuted at some point.

Remember John 17:15 (NKJV), *"I do not pray that You should take them out of the world, but that You should keep them from the evil one."*

The Beginning of Sorrows

So for now it seems that today, at the publishing of this book, we are still in the beginning of sorrows, which is before the third temple and the tribulation and the wrath of satan during the second three and a half years of the seven-year period from the third temple completion. The sorrows will get much more intense during this period with all the signs increasing.

In Matthew 24, the disciples—having heard that Jesus must leave them, and that this second temple will be utterly destroyed—asked Him basically when they, His followers, would see Him again. There were no questions about the rapture, they only knew He was coming back a second time and wanted to know what signposts to look for. Matthew 24:3 (KJV) says, *"And as he sat upon the mount of Olives, the disciples came unto him privately, saying, Tell us, when shall these things be? and what shall be the sign of thy coming, and of the end of the world?"*

Jesus Himself then warns them not to be deceived, as Paul also warned. He gave them signs of false prophets and false messiahs, wars and rumors of war especially concerning Israel, then pestilences. The fact that pestilences is mentioned seems to be significant as pestilence has always been around, but not worldwide at the same time as we have seen today. Then Jesus mentions earthquakes, which again is very significant since earthquakes are somewhat common occurrences. These again are signs His return is getting closer. Then the sorrows increase with persecution of the saints. These signs are the beginning of sorrow but not yet His return.

Jesus tells His disciples the following, recorded in Matthew 24:5-8 (NKJV):

> *For many will come in My name, saying, "I am the Christ," and will deceive many. And you will hear of wars and rumors of wars. See that you are not troubled; for all these things must come to pass, but the end is not yet. For nation will rise against nation, and kingdom against kingdom. And there will be famines, pestilences, and earthquakes in various places. All these are the beginning of sorrows.*

So from the timeline Jesus gives, it looks like the beginning of sorrows ends with these last two verses in Matthew 24:13-14 (NIV):

> *But the one who stands firm to the end will be saved. And this gospel of the kingdom will be preached in the whole world as a testimony to all nations, and then the end will come.*

So basically, we are possibly in the tail end of the beginning of sorrows as we see all these signs increase, including worldwide pestilence, talk of wars (World War III) as never before. There is much false information and an increase of persecution around the world; perhaps not as much yet in the USA and a few other parts of the world, but we know it's coming more and more, along with the great harvest of souls in many nations.

But the greatest sign is that *"this gospel of the kingdom will be preached in the whole world as a testimony to all nations, and then the end will come."*

This is the part I am focusing on—seeing as many people saved as possible. In the past two years, we have seen more souls saved than at any time. I don't focus on any of the negative things in the world, I just see them as signposts showing me how much time I possibly have to win the lost and try to finish the Great Commission. It's a time of great joy and glory and excitement as the best place to be is on offense invading the kingdom of darkness and snatching souls out—and into salvation! That should be our focus as we see the signs increasing.

When does the beginning of sorrows end and the tribulation begin? Well, Jesus mentions the next *big* signpost for us to know when we have shifted out of the beginning of sorrows to a possible seven-year countdown. When we are taken out (raptured) is up for discussion, but it looks very possible we are here to see the third temple and a man declaring himself God, as Jesus tells us to look for this as one of the signposts. If we are no longer here, why would He tell His followers to look for this event. The next verses reveal what the next major signposts are:

> *So when you see standing in the holy place "the abomination that causes desolation," spoken of through the prophet Daniel—let the reader understand—then let those who are in Judea flee to the mountains. Let no one on the housetop go down to take anything out of the house. Let no one in the field go back to get their cloak. How dreadful it will be in those days for pregnant women and nursing mothers! Pray that your flight will not take place in winter or on the Sabbath* (Matthew 24:15-20 NIV).

So even if we are here to see these events as Jesus seems to imply, it's also the most exciting time in world history to be alive as we possibly will be the generation that gets to see the actual soon return of our Messiah Yeshua/Jesus!

There are also some super exciting events after the third temple is profaned by the antichrist. It does not stop there as the two witnesses also come while the antichrist is on earth, challenging him and driving him crazy like a thriller action movie, which is for another book. Things will be very interesting. Even in the hardest days of the wrath of satan during the tribulation, there will still be a witness and the power of God revealed as the Holy Spirit seems to still be moving.

Some say that the Holy Spirit gets removed from the earth with the saints before the antichrist appears. But the Bible talks about great multitudes also coming to the Lord during the tribulation. To be saved you need the Holy Spirit to convict the world of sin. And through the power of the Holy Spirit on earth the great signs and wonders and demonstrations of power will occur, so how could the Holy Spirit be gone but still moving in power and convicting the last harvest to be saved.

On the contrary, there will be many saved and great demonstrations of power even during the tribulation. The two witnesses alone will be moving in great power not seen since the time of Elijah and Moses, apart from the 144,000 and so on.

In Revelation 7, one of the elders is asking who are these saints in Heaven crying out to God,

> *Then one of the elders asked me, "These in white robes—who are they, and where did they come from?" I answered, "Sir, you know." And he said, "These are they who have come out of the great tribulation; they*

> *have washed their robes and made them white in the blood of the Lamb"* (Revelation 7:13-14 NIV).

So even in the great tribulation souls are being saved, Jesus wins, and there is still a witness of the gospel. The Lord does not stop trying to win souls, and many will still come to Him in those days even if it costs them their life. I've read the end of the Book and spoiler alert, God wins!

Jesus does not seem to put on this list that we are taken out of here before the third temple when the antichrist sits in the third temple declaring himself God.

On the contrary, it seems to me that Jesus is still talking and listing in order what will occur, and even instructs the believers to pray that the timing of these events will not be in winter. Does Jesus mean during the tribulation we are to pray that it's not in winter that the man of sin reveals himself when people have to flee? Well, toward the end of the list of what to watch for, including the antichrist, he says this in Matthew 24:29 (NKJV), "*Immediately* ***after the tribulation*** *of those days the sun will be darkened, and the moon will not give its light; the stars will fall from heaven, and the powers of the heavens will be shaken.*"

Tribulation of what days is Jesus referring to? Immediately after what He mentions in Matthew, the actual signposts to look for before His coming, along with satan's wrath against believers and those who won't take the mark of the beast.

Remember, the disciples are asking Jesus when they will see Him again after He leaves them. Jesus then lists for them what believers need to watch for, seemingly indicating believers are here to watch for what will happen. Then He ends the list with "*after the tribulation of those days,*" which are yet to come; but there is no mention here of a sudden rapture before the man of sin and the great falling away. In fact, Jesus says to look for it. What is the grand finale after the tribulation of those days still to come? Matthew 24:30 (NKJV) answers that question for us:

> *Then the sign of the Son of Man will appear in heaven, and then all the tribes of the earth will mourn, and they will see the Son of Man coming on the clouds of heaven with power and great glory.*

This is referring to the final return of the Lord that the disciples were asking about. So if this occurs as it reads, it seems that some things get darker, but the gospel keeps going out brighter and brighter even while many fall away—but many get saved as well. All this keeps going like birth pains leading to the third temple event with the man of sin revealed, then great persecution and wrath, but those who endure to the end will be saved. During the great falling away and the false prophets and false messiahs, a great glory and harvest will also be occurring. This will be a testing time as Daniel was shown: "*Many will be purged, purified (made white) and refined, but the wicked will behave wickedly. None of the wicked shall understand, but those who are [spiritually] wise will understand*" (Daniel 12:10 AMP).

Christ's prophetic outline of future events in Matthew 24 does not contain a pretribulation rapture of the church. On the contrary, the gathering of the elect by God's angels at Christ's Second Coming, at the sound of the trumpet (verse 31), is unmistakably the rapture of the church after the tribulation. "*Immediately after the distress of those days.... Then will appear the sign of the Son of Man in heaven. And all the peoples of the earth will mourn when they see the Son of Man coming on the clouds of heaven, with power and great glory*"

(Matthew 24:29-30 NIV). Luke's parallel description of this apocalyptic redemption confirms this idea: "*When these things begin to take place, stand up and lift up your heads, because your redemption is drawing near*" (Luke 21:28 NIV).

For those who are still alive on earth during this time, Daniel seems to confirm Jesus' words showing the timeline of events; the verse in Daniel 12:10 shows believers being purified during this time of testing. How long are believers tested before the trial is over is revealed in the next two verses. When is the exact timing? Daniel is given the exact timing and sequence of events to know how long the trials lasts:

> *From the time that the regular sacrifice [that is, the daily burnt offering] is taken away and the abomination of desolation is set up [ruining the temple for worship of the true God], there will be 1,290 days* [3.5 years]. *How blessed [happy, fortunate, spiritually prosperous] and beloved is he who waits expectantly [enduring without wavering for the period of tribulation] and comes to the 1,335 days* [3.6 years]! (Daniel 12:11-12 AMP)

So, those who endure to the end will be saved. Endures to the end of what? Most likely if you read it as simply as it says, it's until the end of the tribulation of those days, as Jesus mentioned, and make it to the end of those exact number of days.

Don't forget there is also the prayer to be counted worthy to escape all these things. This does not necessarily mean we are vanished from the earth, but some believers who are here can have supernatural protection and even become unkillable until the Lord returns, just as John being boiled alive and not harmed and Paul being stoned, shipwrecked, and bitten by a venomous snake only to walk away as if nothing happened. Noah and his family were not taken to Heaven but delivered in the midst of the flood. Let's be open to any scenario we find ourselves in and fully trust till the end, not wavering. In the same passages in Matthew 24, right in the middle, Jesus gives a promise: "*But the one who endures and bears up [under suffering] to the end will be saved*" (Matthew 24:13 AMP).

Does the Bible clearly list a rapture first and then a seven-year period and then after that a Second Return? (That almost looks like two returns instead of one.) Let's first read the words of Paul in 1 Thessalonians 4:13-18 (NKJV) as they are, and not through the lens of our favorite end-time theologian without taking away from what is written here:

> *But I do not want you to be ignorant, brethren, concerning those who have fallen asleep, lest you sorrow as others who have no hope. For if we believe that Jesus died and rose again, even so God will bring with Him those who sleep in Jesus. For this we say to you by the word of the Lord,* ***that we who are alive and remain until the coming of the Lord*** *will by no means precede those who are asleep. For the Lord Himself will descend from heaven with a shout, with the voice of an archangel, and with the trumpet of God. And the dead in Christ will rise first. Then we who are alive and remain shall be caught up together with them in the clouds to meet the Lord in the air. And thus we shall always be with the Lord. Therefore comfort one another with these words.*

Notice the words "*that we who are alive and remain* ***until the coming*** *of the Lord.*" That is referring to the Second Coming.

The coming is the second return of the Lord to earth. It does not say "you who remain at the first part of the rapture waiting for part two of the Second Coming." Throughout the Bible it refers to *one* Second Coming, otherwise it would clearly mention it as two parts spread out.

Many like to separate the Second Coming into two stages of a rapture, then a seven-year period then another Second Coming. Nowhere is this taught in the Scriptures. His first coming was in one stage (the incarnation), and so will be His Second Coming.

Notice 1 Thessalonians 4 verse 17: *"Then we which are alive and remain shall be* ***caught up****"* (Strong's Greek #726); the term *caught up* means "to seize or to catch away by force." We will be caught up together in the clouds, *"to meet the Lord in the air and so shall we ever be with the Lord."* The passage does not say anything about us going to Heaven. It only says we are caught up to meet the Lord in the air (Strong's Greek #109). This term *air* is precisely the same word Paul used in 1 Corinthians 9:26 (KJV), *"I therefore, so run not as uncertainly; so fight I, not as one that beateth the air,"* meaning the actual air that surrounds us. Nowhere does the passage speak of us going to Heaven. Actually it says we will have an encounter with the Lord in the air.

Second Timothy 4:1 (KJV) declares, *"I charge thee therefore before God, and the Lord Jesus Christ, who shall judge the quick and the dead at his appearing and his kingdom."* His appearing is the same as His coming.

The term *judge* (Strong's Greek #2919) is to determine or decide; in this case, regarding the quick and the dead (Strong's Greek #2198 to be alive), which can be translated *corpse* at His appearing (Strong's Greek #4430), specifically, the one second return of Christ and His Kingdom. So if you read this literally, it says God will pass final judgment on the church, the dead and living, at His appearing and kingdom. When He comes again it will be to resurrect the dead in Christ, catch away the living to meet the Lord in the air, and then establish an earthly kingdom.

Paul does not differentiate between a rapture and a Second Advent. It simply reads *"at His appearing and kingdom."* When He comes again, it will be to resurrect the dead in Christ, catch away the living to meet the Lord Himself in the air, and then establish an earthly kingdom.

I, of course, would prefer that He comes before the tribulation and not have to have our faith tested, but that's not how the Bible says it will happen.

If you were to be mistaken in the timing, it's better to have been mistaken thinking He will come later and be willing to be tested and not deny the Lord—than to assume we won't be tested and won't be here for the events Jesus, Paul, and the prophets clearly describe to look for and be caught unprepared.

When Christians trust in the teaching that they will be raptured to Heaven before the persecution of the antichrist, how will they be prepared for the coming final test of faith? The danger of pretribulationism is that it instills in the hearts of God's people a false hope and thus fails to prepare the church for her final crisis and triumph.

Revelation 2:7 (NLT) says, *"To the one who is victorious, I will give the right to eat from the tree of life, which is in the paradise of God."*

I know this is a lot to take in for some people, but I also know that sometimes we can just take things for granted and accept things we are told without actually searching it out ourselves.

Before 1948, most of the church worldwide did not believe in an actual physical Israel returning as a nation. They would read the word *Israel* thinking it meant the church, since Israel had not been a nation for 2,000 years. So they just spiritualized the word *Israel* to mean the church, which was a huge error. Most thought we replaced Israel. Then in 1948, a major paradigm shift had to be seriously considered by the most revered scholars and most devoted churchgoers alike. Even if most were good men and women of God, their understanding of the end times had to change with the current reality of Israel being recognized as a nation.

I'm not dogmatic, as no one knows the day or the hour, but I'm saying let's be open to the fact that we may still be here for at least part of these events that Jesus Himself told His disciples to watch for.

Revelation 14:9-13 (NKJV) reveals to us:

> *Then a third angel followed them, saying with a loud voice, "If anyone worships the beast and his image, and receives his mark on his forehead or on his hand, he himself shall also drink of the wine of the wrath of God, which is poured out full strength into the cup of His indignation. He shall be tormented with fire and brimstone in the presence of the holy angels and in the presence of the Lamb. And the smoke of their torment ascends forever and ever; and they have no rest day or night, who worship the beast and his image, and whoever receives the mark of his name." Here is the patience of the saints; here are those who keep the commandments of God and the faith of Jesus.*
>
> *Then I heard a voice from heaven saying to me, "Write: 'Blessed are the dead who die in the Lord from now*

> *on.'" "Yes," says the Spirit, "that they may rest from their labors, and their works follow them."*

Not every faithful believer will die, of course—the Scriptures are clear some disciples will remain alive until the coming of the Lord (1 Thessalonians 4:15-17; 1 Corinthians 15:51; Matthew 24:22,31). Verse 12 to me stands out as a contrast, particularly, *"those who keep the commandments of God and the faith of Jesus."* I can imagine people receiving the mark, telling themselves, "God knows my heart that I really worship Him. I'm just doing this out of necessity."

Could Revelation 3:10 refer to a pretribulation gathering? Such a thing is certainly not explicitly taught there.

One passage often promoted as a pretribulation rapture is 1 Thessalonians 4:15-18 (NKJV):

> *For this we say to you by the word of the Lord, that we who are alive and remain until the coming of the Lord will by no means precede those who are asleep. For the Lord Himself will descend from heaven with a shout, with the voice of an archangel, and with the trumpet of God. And the dead in Christ will rise first. Then we who are alive and remain shall be caught up together with them in the clouds to meet the Lord in the air. And thus we shall always be with the Lord. Therefore comfort one another with these words.*

There are two groups of believers—those who are alive and remain until the coming of the Lord, and those who are asleep (physically dead). The resurrection occurs first. Then those who are alive and remain will be caught up together with the resurrected believers in the clouds to meet the Lord in the air. The context of the first resurrection (Revelation 20:1-6) is after the tribulation, thus the gathering of 1 Thessalonians 4:17 is also after the tribulation.

The Bible does not contradict itself.

If you read the Bible without reading someone else's opinion or commentary into it, God's Word will open your eyes. The Bible was meant to be understood by the simple reader. For example, the Bible says you shall heal the sick and prophesy, but cessationists say these works of God ceased. But the Bible does not say that. You don't need an "expert" to tell you what the Bible "really means." Read God's Word and let God's Word read you.

When Christians trust in the teaching that they will be raptured to Heaven before the persecution of the antichrist, how will they be prepared for the coming final test of faith? As mentioned previously, the danger of pretribulationism is that it instills in the hearts of God's people a false hope and thus fails to prepare the church for her final crisis.

I don't want you to lose your faith in the end times when things don't pan out as you thought it was supposed to, thinking, *Well, what else have I been taught that is wrong?* Many might think along these lines and then throw out their entire belief system and be tempted to leave the faith due to timeline errors. Most Christians just leave it up to those who "specialize" in end-time prophecy without digging into the Word of God themselves, thinking it's too complicated. The Bible actually promises a blessing just for reading the book of Revelation. Now is a good time to read this timely book as it refers more to our day than any other.

The Bible is 100 percent accurate—it's just that our interpretation of it may not always be 100 percent, and then our understanding can shift based on actual events occurring that the Bible mentioned and may show us that a possible change is necessary in our perceived timeline of events.

On another note. These major events are in the works right now and will advance unless something slows them down.

For instance, the emergence of Central Bank Digital Currency (CBDC). An informative article about CBDC states that only a few countries (including Bahamas, Nigeria, Jamaica) have "fully launched a digital currency" but "despite the potential benefits of a US CBDC, it remains a concept for now. …and the Fed has still not indicated that they are in any hurry to launch a CBDC."[9]

The Stargate Initiative (an artificial intelligence (AI) infrastructure) is planning to be fully funded by 2029 with $500 billion, which President Trump announced January 24, 2025. This would be the AI super-infrastructure platform that would also be used for the worldwide digital currency system.[10] Can we slow this down?

Slow Down the Timeline

So when the Jews in or near Jerusalem do have to run to the Judean mountains when the antichrist declares himself God, and believers worldwide have to also stand against this beast and this antichrist system, an interesting phrase from Scripture will occur to the believer, "*Pray that when you flee, it will not be in the winter*" (Matthew 24:40 NASB). So it's possible that our prayers will affect the timeline and slow down time and end-time events. If it's possible to pray that this event does not occur at a certain a time, what other events can we slow down to give us more time to win the lost or pray that the timing is changed.

We see that Nineveh (see Jonah 3) was to be destroyed, but God gave the Ninevites at least another generation after reconsidering. We see that Sodom and Gomorrah could have been spared if God could find even 10 righteous, which He could not (see Genesis 18:20-33). Hezekiah was able to change the timeline of his life and get 15 more years (see Isaiah 38:5). Certain things must and eventually will happen, but prayer and repentance and prophecy can slow down the timeline of some events that must happen and even alter others unmentioned in the Bible, events that seem inevitable, without changing course.

We need to get involved and work with God in these end times! God wants us to redeem time, not waste these precious few years that we may have left to do His will and expand His Kingdom, winning as many souls as possible and discipling nations before His return. It seems time is running out, but when Joshua needed a little more daylight to win the battle, God had him pray to stop time and command the sun to stand still for 24 more hours and it actually did!

Using NASA data, it has been reported some years ago that there was a 24-hour gap missing in time.[11] There are also reports of nations writing that it was dark on the other side of the world for 24 hours during the same time Israel had light.

During World War II when it looked like Hitler would conquer England and eventually the rest of Europe, intercessor Rees Howells[12] locked himself up in a room in London and began to intercede for his country. He knew England was not ready for an onslaught from Germany at that time. Hitler was about to invade England when he suddenly changed his mind and went instead to Eastern Europe. This changed the progress of the war, allowing England time to arm itself, as the country would have been totally defeated if Hitler had attacked England earlier on. This would have eventually led to Hitler seizing all of Europe. I believe that the battle was shifted due to prayer warriors and intercessors. Likewise, it's time now more than ever to pray for our nation and Israel. There are plans in many nations to try and overtake the United States of America.

China has a plan, as do terrorists and other nations forming alliances, to try to conquer the USA. I believe they will try, but prayer will push them back at least for a season, which should be a major wake-up call for our nation. Many revered revivalists and men of God in the days of former revivals saw similar warnings over America.

Only prayer, repentance, and a great move of God can shift these plans so that the USA remains a sheep nation under God and stands with Israel to the end, despite the shakings and judgments that must hit the earth in certain areas.

I believe that Donald Trump's second term as president has slowed down many of the negative events that would have increased and accelerated faster had he not been elected a second time, including speeding up some of the end-time wars. America for sure would have been quickly turned into a communist/socialist type of governmental system, suffocating the church.

I believe God has given the USA and the world a pause in time due to prayer worldwide. What will we do with these next few years? Will we go all out for the Lord and spread the gospel—or will we take for granted the extra bonus years He has given us to accomplish our destiny as a nation and a people without the extra hardship of much greater persecution? There will still be great shaking and a normal increase in persecution both in America and the world, but it will be a shaking until harvest to get people to look up to Jesus. We can no longer just go about our lives focused solely on our self-interests. We must live life with Him, for Him. It's a redemptive shaking to awaken!

What Do We Do Now?

It's like the prophet who told the king to strike the ground. He was in a *kairos* moment just as we are in now. The king lazily struck the ground only three times. The prophet was upset and rebuked him for not striking the ground with more zeal for at least six or seven times, as that's how many more times he would have had victory over his enemies.

Are we discerning this grace and extra lease on time that God has given America, Israel, and the church worldwide? Or will we be asleep at the wheel as many were after the 2016 US election, squandering the favor we had, and go back to seeing our nation overrun by evil global elites, thus speeding up the worst of the end times—or will we redeem this time?

Let's make it the best for Jesus and extend the time as much as possible to finish the Great Commission, seeing both Israel and the nations have the full number of souls saved that our Messiah is worthy of seeing in honor of His sacrificial death and resurrection for the entire world.

This is the time to go for it! Whatever God has told you to do, do it now! The harvest is ripe but the laborers are few (see Matthew 9:37; Luke 10:2). Pray for more laborers. Become a laborer! There will be so many souls saved that the biggest issue won't be getting people saved but finding enough people to share the gospel to those ready to be saved and finding enough laborers to disciple and pastor the multitudes who will be coming into the Kingdom of God.

We are the generation that will see the most exciting times in world history along with the chaos in the world—but also the fullness of the end-time Glory of God along with the end-time harvest in these last days! Many of us may even see the return of our Lord and Savior in these exciting end times!

I do believe that we will be physically changed in a twinkling of an eye and that there is a rapture of the saints, but the timeline might not be what many think or hope it will be. It is just not listed in what Jesus said or in what Daniel recorded. The rapture does occur, just not in the timeline many tout—otherwise wouldn't Jesus and Daniel have mentioned it occurring before the man of sin sits in the temple to defile it? Could it be that the moment of Jesus' one and only Second Coming is when we are changed in a twinkling of an eye, raptured for a microsecond and then start the new millennium with Jesus sitting in the temple in Jerusalem?

Again, if you read it simply without someone else telling you what they think it means, but read it as it's written, it seems the blessed hope is not necessarily being raptured, though that does occur. The great hope is His soon Second Coming! The blessed hope ultimately is being born again and knowing that we will spend eternity with Him—whether we live or die we will be with Him. Paul says in essence, "To live is Christ, to die is gain so either way we win!" (See Philippians 1:21.)

> *For the Lord himself will come down from heaven, with a loud command, with the voice of the archangel and with the trumpet call of God, and the dead in Christ will rise first. After that,* ***we who are still alive and are left*** *be caught up with them in the clouds to meet the Lord in the air. And so we will be with the Lord forever* (1 Thessalonians 4:16-17 NIV).

If the Lord could rapture us at any moment right now, then why does it say, "*we who are still alive*"? It's because much of the earth during the tribulation will be killed, but we who are still alive and remain counted worthy to escape all these trials and persecutions, will be changed in a moment.

What if *"we who are still alive and are left"* means we who have not been killed by the antichrist, and have not died of pestilence, war, and natural disasters during the *"tribulation of those days"* but escaped all these things? Jesus mentioned those *"who endure till the end will be saved,"* and we who still remain on earth seems to mean those of us still here are then caught up and changed.

Why would it need to say, *"for those who still remain"*? Because much of the earth's population will be killed as the Bible gives different percentages like one-fourth die of this and two-thirds of this and that. That seems to be telling believers, "You who survived all this and held true to My word, enduring and praying to be counted worthy to escape all these things." (Note: many also will be called to be martyrs or die of old age and that is just as noble and takes just as much if not more faith; also it will be for those God is leading to stay alive till His return to also trust Him for this, depending on the call and conviction God has given each one.)

> *Listen, I tell you a mystery: We will not all sleep, but we will all be changed—in a flash, in the twinkling of an eye, at the last trumpet. For the trumpet will sound, the dead will be raised imperishable, and we will be changed. ...then the saying that is written will come true: "Death has been swallowed up in victory"* (1 Corinthians 15:51-54 NIV).

The mystery is that not all will be killed, but God will supernaturally allow a remnant to escape all these things on earth to see His actual Second Coming. Those who endure to the end will be caught up in a twinkling of a microsecond and have new uncorrupted bodies for the millennium.

12

THE FATHER'S GLORY

I have had years of experience with the Glory of God and taught on the Glory of God for many years, ever since I came into contact with a prophetess years ago named Ruth Heflin during her camp meeting revivals in Ashland, Virginia.

Before that, I believe I had gone in and out of glory mixed with anointing. Once you've crossed past anointing to glory, you know you are in a different place. Going past the anointing on my life and into Heaven's Glory revolutionized everything. It has totally changed my life. But in 2018, I stumbled onto the highest level of glory that I know of, the Father's Glory! It felt like being born again, again.

Often as believers, of course, we know Jesus at salvation and the power of His blood, His salvation, and the glory of His person and His name. Then many go on to experience the power and glory of the infilling of the Holy Spirit and start to then experience healing, deliverance, praying in the Spirit, and the prophetic realm. Also many know the Holy Spirit as the Comforter and friend, not just an invisible power but the person of the Holy Spirit. For most, they stop there.

Then beyond that, many believers will pay homage to Father God using His name in prayer as Jesus taught us. But most don't go beyond that. Most believers don't have an intimate relationship with the Father. Often people subconsciously have a fear of getting close to God the Father. But if they do get close to Him, they may experience some level of the Father known as the Father's Love. This was a very real move of God in the early 1990s.

I experienced the Father's love after having visited the revival in Toronto. I was a missionary living in Europe at the time, and one day I had a powerful encounter with the Father's love. I suddenly knew Him in a way I never truly knew Him before in actuality, only in doctrine. I would weep for hours in the presence of the Father's love that would fill the room. This set me free from the fear of and the need for people's validation that I was doing a good job. All those chains broke and it was just me and God, and all was for Him. This was in 1993. From there my ministry soared, and we saw many years of revival meetings.

After that I experienced the fire of the Pensacola revival, once again pouring out my heart and running to His fire of holiness and fearlessness to share the gospel in a new way. From there we saw new extended revivals that would go as long as weeks up to six months straight, internationally where we were based and in the US.

But in 2018 I stumbled upon the highest level of God's Glory I have ever experienced. This was even beyond the Father's love. The love of the Father will set you free from religiosity and pleasing people, but the Father's Glory is the *fullness* of the Father, which is the only way I can describe it with human words. I discovered not just the Father's love, which I knew, but went one step further to discover a portion of the Father's Glory.

It started when my good friend, Warren Marcus, an executive producer of the *It's Supernatural* television program hosted by Sid Roth, called me. He was so excited as he had found a new revelation. He kept trying to explain it to me over the phone, but he shared so many things so fast and excitedly that I couldn't catch fully what he was trying to convey. He wrote a book about it shortly afterward, and I asked him to send me a copy.[13] I devoured the book and step by step prayed in a totally different way, waiting on the Father of Glory to step in. What happened next changed my life yet again in an epic way.

For about 50 days in my daily prayer time, I would be caught up in the Father's Glory for hours at a time all while just praying a few lines then pausing and waiting, then continuing in prayer and waiting. I was praying the only prayer in the Bible the Father Himself gave to humankind to pray, which I will explain a bit later in this chapter.

We know that Adam and Eve had perfect direct fellowship with God in the Garden of Eden. Then man sinned and that relationship was broken. There had to be a blood sacrifice to atone for that sin over and over again due to that break in relationship—until Jesus came and became the final sacrifice. The whole point of sending Jesus to die for our sins is not only so we could be saved, but also to renew our relationship with the Father. Jesus is the door, the way.

Too many people think He is just the door to get into Heaven. But Jesus is actually the doorway back to the Father. Most people know this biblically, but most have never experienced the glory of the Father.

Imagine Moses saying he wanted to see God's face and climbed the mountain only to see His back, which was enough for Moses' face to shine like the sun. The whole story of humanity is of the Father trying to reconnect with His children.

It's funny how we often sing songs in church such as, "I just want to see Your face," followed by a message saying, "No one can see the face of God Himself and live, but then again King David said, 'Your face will I seek.'" So which is it? In the Old

Testament passages this was very true. Even just touching the ark of the covenant or the wheels carrying it the wrong way could cause you to drop dead.

In the New Testament at the Cross, God ripped in half the thick heavy curtain that was in the temple separating the priest from the Holy Place to the Holy of Holies at the moment of Jesus' death. The curtain literally tore in half that day in Jerusalem when Jesus became the sacrificial Lamb saying, *"It is finished."* This tearing apart signified that not only the high priest once a year could get that close to the Father, but through the blood of Jesus, we also have access to the Father in a new way.

When Moses asked to see His face, God replied, *"But you cannot see my face, for no one may see me and live"* (Exodus 33:20 NIV). Then God hid Moses in the cleft of the rock and passed by, but He only allowed Moses to see His back, not His face (Exodus 33:21-23 NIV). God explicitly told Moses why he could not see His face when He said, *"No one can see me and live."* Therefore, we may understand from this statement that it is out of love for us that He hides His face, because it is necessary for our survival.

We may ask why our survival depends on it, and why we would die if we saw His face. I realize that the holiness and power of God have a lot to do with that. The prophet Isaiah attempted to describe the indescribable scenes around the throne when he saw the Lord seated there high and lifted up.

> *In the year of King Uzziah's death I saw the Lord sitting on a throne, lofty and exalted, with the train of His robe filling the temple. Seraphim were standing above Him, each having six wings: with two each covered his face, and with two each covered his feet, and with two each flew. And one called out to another and said,*

> *"Holy, Holy, Holy, is the* Lord *of armies. The whole earth is full of His glory." And the foundations of the thresholds trembled at the voice of him who called out, while the temple was filling with smoke. Then I said, "Woe to me, for I am ruined! Because I am a man of unclean lips, and I live among a people of unclean lips; for my eyes have seen the King, the* Lord *of armies"* (Isaiah 6:1-5 NASB).

Did you notice how Isaiah knew he was ruined when his eyes beheld the King on His throne, the Lord of armies/hosts? I'm sure you or I would feel the same way if we saw God the Father, too. John the apostle described a similar sight when he was taken up in the Spirit to Heaven and stood before the throne:

> *Immediately I was in the Spirit; and behold, a throne set in heaven, and One sat on the throne. And He who sat there was like a jasper and a sardius stone in appearance; and there was a rainbow around the throne, in appearance like an emerald* (Revelation 4:2-3 NKJV).

It's amazing how the luminescent smoke fills the temple during those times of worship, as the light and the glory emanate from God, who is seated upon His throne. John describes it as a rainbow around the throne in appearance like an emerald. Apparently there are lovely bands of colors in the streams of light and glory surrounding Him. God wraps Himself in light as with a garment (Psalm 104:2 NIV). He enshrouds His head with this glory fog so that you cannot see His face. It's awesome to behold and extraordinarily beautiful. In fact, He is perfect in beauty, unlike anyone or anything else you have ever seen or ever will see. Scripture says, "*Out of Zion comes the excellence of His beauty"* (Psalm 50:2 Brenton Septuagint). Other translations refer to it as *"the perfection of beauty."*

Often we sense that the cloud of glory is in a place. That means that His face can also be hidden in that cloud. Some of the most powerful corporate visitations I've been a part of was at Ruth Heflin's campground in Ashland as the thick, physical cloud filled the meeting. Someone had opened a side door, I went outside to see if this was really what I was seeing. When I stepped outside to look back inside, I could only see thick clouds in the room; I could not even see the people. The glory realm was the strongest I had ever experienced in a room. It felt like we were all transported to Heaven.

The apostle Paul had also seen the Lord when Jesus appeared to him at noontime while he was on the road to Damascus. At that time, the Lord appeared brighter than the noonday sun. Paul had also been caught up to Paradise and heard inexpressible words that he was not permitted to speak. He described God like this:

> ...*God, the blessed and only Ruler, the King of kings and Lord of lords, who alone is immortal and who lives in unapproachable light, whom no one has seen or can see. To him be honor and might forever. Amen* (1 Timothy 6:15-16 NIV).

David said, "*One thing I ask from the LORD, this only do I seek: that I may dwell in the house of the LORD all the days of my life, to gaze on the beauty of the LORD and to seek him in his temple*" (Psalm 27:4 NIV). David's one desire was to behold the beauty of the Lord.

One of the most exciting events in human history will be when Jesus returns and we see Him on the earth face to face.

But guess who else will be on the earth with Him. Father God!

That realization blew me away, as I had never been taught this. But God Himself did come on the earth before and dwelt in the Holy of Holies and the priests did interact with God the Father as well as many other mighty men of God in the past.

Knowing this, why would it be a stretch to believe that the Father would come during the millennium when Jesus returns to earth. Heaven is amazing because the Father and Son are both there, so how much more exciting when we will be on earth with our new heavenly bodies during the millennium as the Father is also here? Our heavenly Father loves His kids; He would not want to be away from us for 1,000 years. All the dead in Christ will rise and the millennium will be beyond imagination, especially knowing the Father and Son will be in Jerusalem at their earthly throne.

Moses' face shone so proudly after getting closer to the Father's Glory than any human on earth. Jesus shined brightly on the mount of transfiguration and Stephen the martyr also shined so brightly, most likely having encounters with the Father's Glory.

Imagine if I told you behind a particular door is *God the Father Himself*, and I asked if you would like to meet Him now. Perhaps a holy terror and the fear of God would seize you, rightly so. You may have a different response if I told you that *Jesus* is behind the door and asked if you would like to meet with Him now. You would probably be overjoyed but with a respectful fear of the Lord. I believe our response to meeting the Father would be different from meeting Jesus.

In fact, most the prophets said they were *undone* or felt like they could die or were a dead man for even looking toward the Father. In the Bible, the phrase *"fell on my face as though dead"* appears in several passages. One notable instance is in Revelation 1:17, where John the apostle falls at the feet of Jesus as though dead, but Jesus reassures him with the words, "*Fear not.*" Another example is found in Ezekiel 1:28, where Ezekiel falls on his face upon seeing the likeness of the glory of Jehovah. Additionally, Daniel 10:9 describes Daniel falling on his face in deep sleep with his face to the ground when he encounters a divine being.

So after the Cross and when Jesus returns, will people be able to visit the Father here on earth? Will He actually be here with Jesus?

Revelation 21:3-4 (NIV) says,

> *And I heard a loud voice from the throne saying, "**Look! God's dwelling place is now among the people,** and he will dwell with them. They will be his people, and God himself will be with them and be their God. He will wipe every tear from their eyes. There will be no more death' or mourning or crying or pain, for the old order of things has passed away."*

The Name of God

The following few paragraphs summarize what I read in my friend Warren Marcus' book, *The Priestly Prayer of the Blessing* (from memory, not verbatim). For centuries religious Jewish rabbis would never dare to try to pronounce the name of God as it was too holy. The closest they get to the name is to write it out with four letters: *YVHV.* Recently archaeologist discoveries have found the high priests ephod and other items with the name of God Himself written. The final verdict is that the closest we can get to knowing the name and pronouncing it is between these two names: (1) *Yahveh* (as opposed to *Yahweh* commonly used.) And (2) *Jehova* pronounced with a y like *Yehova.* In the past I've heard it said that the closest name is *Yav He Vav He,* which is the closest to the *YVHV* spelling. So I started to use His name *Yahveh* when I pray to the Father in Jesus/Yeshua's name.

The name in which you worship God often causes the meaning of that name to manifest. When you worship the God of Healing using the name *Jehova Rapha,* it can start to activate the healing power of God. The same goes for using in prayer the name of God the Provider *Jehova Jireh,* and so forth. So imagine when you seek the face of God and use the closest to His original name feared by even the most religious rabbis, *Yehova* or *Yawveh.*

Next, I started to pray the only prayer in the Bible Father God Himself gave us to pray, mentioned earlier in the chapter along with *The Priestly Prayer of the Blessing.* This prayer is one of the most powerful prayers in the entire Bible. In fact, it was so powerful that Aaron the high priest would pray this over the children of Israel every year on the highest holy days of the year. It is so powerful that even Constantine—when he took over the church after Rome destroyed Jerusalem—forbid believing Jews to pray this prayer over believers as it would release great power and blessing in their lives, which somehow he was against as anti-Jewish sentiment was strong toward anything that seemed Jewish after the destruction of Jerusalem.

Constantine also forbade the Gentile church from even fellowshipping with Jews and also forbade celebrating feasts such as Passover and reading the Old Testament. When that occurred, the Gentile church lost immense revelation until the Bible was finally printed again and believers could read the entire Bible for themselves, leading to the gradual restoration of all the church had lost since the early church. This is one of those revelations.

The prayer I'm referring to is the Aaronic Blessing, also known as the priestly prayer. I have known this prayer and verse in English, but the power of it never really hit me until I read the newly discovered full translation of it from the original Hebrew back into the Amplified English to get the full meaning. As I would praise and worship then start to pray this prayer over myself, sometimes I would only get to one verse and the Father's Glory would overtake me for who knows how long, releasing indescribable glory, revelation, and acceleration. In fact at the end of 50 days, God had accelerated our life and ministry in so many blessed ways. (I discovered the Aaronic blessing prayer in Warren Marcus' book *The Priestly Prayer of the Blessing.*)

Within weeks, God told us to move from Sedona, in northern Arizona, to the capital of Arizona, in the Phoenix area. He told me, like King David, the glory needed to be in the capital as when David was to take the ark to Jerusalem, not leave it in Obadiah's home.

After moving, we were soon organizing the largest stadium event I had ever organized in the USA. We held a major historic event at the 50,000-seat Sun Devil Stadium, of all places, at Arizona State University. Thousands were healed and saved as both Christian and secular media covered the event. It was the only Christian evangelistic stadium event in 2020 and beyond, as the pandemic came just weeks after. This glory and the effects of it has not stopped. I had recently preached to more than 1 million people in two nights as well as in many other national events—and His blessings keep expanding as does the Glory of God.

For *all* have sinned and come short of His Glory. That means every human at one time knew the glory at least when they were a spirit before they were born. In Jeremiah 1:5 (NIV) God tells us, *"Before I formed you in the womb I knew you, before you were born I set you apart; I appointed you as a prophet to the nations."* How did God know him before he was even formed in the womb? That's a deep revelation right there and could be another entire book. When people get saved who have never heard the gospel, they often say, "This is what I was looking for," or, "I feel like I'm back home now where I belong."

How could this be unless the spirit part of humans once knew the glory and the Father, and when they get saved and their spirit is reborn the memories in their spirit come back to life and they get a glimpse of the memory of what they lost. *"All have sinned and come short of the glory."* So if all lost the glory, then at one time all had a sense of the glory at least in their spiritual self, which is breathed from Heaven upon birth giving us life. Just as when someone dies that same human spirit departs as they exhale their last breath.

That same God of Glory, the heavenly Father wants the whole world to know Him once again and accept His Son Jesus so they can be saved and have eternal life with Them in Heaven.

The Father's Glory Prayer

Also known as the Aaronic Blessing, in English it reads:

> *The* L*ORD* *bless you, and keep you;*
> *The* L*ORD* *make His face shine upon you,*
> *and be gracious to you;*
> *The* L*ORD* *lift up His countenance upon you,*
> *and give you peace.*
>
> (Numbers 6:24-26 NKJV)

The following is an Amplified Hebrew to English interpretation and translation of this passage in Numbers 6. Each phrase from the common version you just read is in bold, followed by the Amplified Hebrew to English translation. As you read each line slowly and pause to meditate on it (and wait on the Father's Glory and revelation), you will be filled with a fuller, deeper understanding of the power, love, and glory of the Father like never before; and while using His name *Yahveh* and ending it with praying in the name of *Yeshua* (Jesus) our Messiah Lord and Savior, you'll experience a glorious transformation.

THE LORD BLESS YOU

May YHWH (HE who exists) kneel before you (making Himself available to you as your HEAVENLY FATHER) so HE can bestow upon you His promises and gifts.

AND KEEP YOU

And GUARD YOU with a HEDGE of THORNY PROTECTION that will prevent satan and all your enemies from harming you. May HE protect your body, soul, mind, and spirit, your loved ones and all your possessions.

THE LORD MAKE HIS FACE SHINE UPON YOU

May YHWH (HE who exists) illuminate the WHOLENESS of HIS BEING toward you, continually bringing to you order, so that you will fulfill your God-given destiny and purpose.

AND BE GRACIOUS TO YOU

May YHWH (HE who exists) provide you with PERFECT LOVE and FELLOWSHIP (never leaving you) and giving you SUSTENANCE (provision) and FRIENDSHIP.

THE LORD LIFT UP HIS COUNTENANCE UPON YOU

May YHWH (HE who exists) LIFT UP and carry His FULLNESS of being toward you (bringing everything that He has to your aid) supporting YOU with His DIVINE EMBRACE and His ENTIRE BEING.

AND GIVE YOU PEACE.

May YHWH (HE Who Exists) set in place all YOU need to be WHOLE and COMPLETE so you can walk in victory, moment by moment, by the power of the Holy Spirit. May HE give you supernatural health, peace, welfare, safety, soundness, tranquility, prosperity, perfection, fullness, rest, harmony, as well as the absence of agitation and discord.

The Father longs to have a closer relationship with His children, which is only through His Son, Jesus. I pray that you seek the face of God the Father like never before. Even if you never see His face but maybe only get ever closer to Him, I know you will be transformed in every way as you pursue knowing God in fullness and honoring Jesus—and knowing the Father as Jesus knew His Father.

Jesus tells us in John 17:21-23 (NLT):

> *I pray that they will all be one, just as you and I are one—as you are in me, Father, and I am in you. And may they be in us so that the world will believe you sent me. I have given them the glory you gave me, so they may be one as we are one. I am in them and you are in me. May they experience such perfect unity that the world will know that you sent me and that you love them as much as you love me.*

ENDNOTES

1 Edwin Orr, "Prayer brings revival," *Evangelical Times*, April 2, 2010; https://www.evangelical-times.org/prayer-brings-revival/; accessed January 29, 2025.

2 Ibid.

3 Gordon C. Olson, "The Secret of Success In The Ministry of Charles G. Finney," *Library of Theology*, https://libraryoftheology.wordpress.com/2019/02/12/the-secret-of-success-in-the-ministry-of-charles-g-finney-by-gordon-c-olson/; accessed January 30, 2025.

4 Ibid.

5 "John G. Lake: Bubonic Plague Testimony," *Pentecostaltheology.com*, March 25, 2020; https://www.pentecostaltheology.com/john-g-lake-bubonic-plague-testimony/; accessed January 31, 2025.

6 For more information, check out this interesting podcast featuring John DeSouza: https://youtu.be/uX4sPWOh3EM?si=ljbRVPRL4rDSNFbN; accessed February 23, 2025.

7 Scharl van Staden, "Engaging the Frequency of Heaven," *Throne Room Mystic*, May 5, 2020; https://throneroommystic.com/engaging-the-frequency-of-heaven; accessed February 24, 2025.

8 Darrell L. Bock, *Luke 9:51-24:53 (Baker Exegetical Commentary on the new Testament)* (Baker Academic 1996), 1691-1692.

9 David Rodeck and Michael Adams, "Digital Currency: The Future of Your Money," *Forbes.com,* May 13, 2024; https://www.forbes.com/advisor/investing/cryptocurrency/digital-currency/; accessed February 8, 2025.

10 Bernard Marr, "What Does Trump's $500 Billion Stargate Mean For The World of AI?" *Forbes.com,* January 23, 2025; https://www.forbes.com/sites/bernardmarr/2025/01/23/what-does-trumps-500-billion-stargate mean-for-the-world-of-ai/; accessed February 23, 2025.

11 TOI Staff, "Eclipse 'stopped the sun' for biblical Joshua, Israeli scientists say," *The Times of Israel,* January 16, 2017; https://www.timesofisrael.com/eclipse-stopped-the-sun-for-biblical-joshua-israeli-scientists-say/; accessed February 23, 2025. See also: David Sedley, "Joshua stopped the sun 3,244 years ago today, scientists say," *The Times of Israel,* October 30, 2017; https://www.timesofisrael.com/3224-years-later-scientists-see-first-ever-recorded-eclipse-in-joshuas-battle/; accessed February 23, 2025.

12 For more information about Rees Howells: Rees Howells and Mathew Backholer, *Rees Howells, Life of Faith, Intercession, Spiritual Warfare and Walking in the Spirit* (Byfaith Media, 2025).

13 Warren M. Marcus, *The Priestly Prayer of the Blessing: The Ancient Secret of the Only Prayer in the Bible Written by God Himself* (Charisma House, 2018).

ABOUT DAVID HERZOG

David Herzog is the cofounder of The Glory Zone Ministries and Awaken2020. David has an evangelistic, prophetic, and teaching ministry and extensive revelation on living and operating in the Glory of God and seeing national awakening. He is the author of nine books including *Glory Invasion, Limitless Glory, and Secrets of the Glory.* He has been a guest on numerous TV shows including *It's Supernatural,* TBN, Daystar and the *FoxNews* channel.

David and his wife, Stephanie, are based in Phoenix, Arizona, and have been in full-time ministry for more than 33 years. They have lived 12 years on the mission field. David and Stephanie have ministered in more than 70 nations in large national evangelistic stadiums, hosting and speaking in conferences, churches, revivals, and outreaches seeing incredible healings, miracles, signs and wonders, and deliverances confirming the gospel message.